Legalized Gambling

Legalized Gambling

OTHER BOOKS OF RELATED INTEREST

Legalized Gambling

David M. Haugen, *Book Editor*

Bruce Glassman, *Vice President*
Bonnie Szumski, *Publisher*
Helen Cothran, *Managing Editor*

Contemporary Issues
Companion

GREENHAVEN PRESS
An imprint of Thomson Gale, a part of The Thomson Corporation

Detroit • New York • San Francisco • San Diego • New Haven, Conn.
Waterville, Maine • London • Munich

LIBRARY OF CONGRESS CATALOGING-IN-PUBLICATION DATA

Legalized gambling / David M. Haugen, book editor.
    p. cm. — (Contemporary issues companion)
    Includes bibliographical references and index.
    ISBN 0-7377-2460-9 (lib. : alk. paper) — ISBN 0-7377-2461-7 (pbk. : alk. paper)
        1. Gambling—United States. 2. Gambling—Law and legislation—United States.
    I. Haugen, David M., 1969– . II. Series.
    HV6715.L43 2006
    363.4'2'0973—dc22

                                                                            2005046129

Printed in the United States of America

CONTENTS

FOREWORD

In the news, on the streets, and in neighborhoods, individuals are confronted with a variety of social problems. Such problems may affect people directly: A young woman may struggle with depression, suspect a friend of having bulimia, or watch a loved one battle cancer. And even the issues that do not directly affect her private life—such as religious cults, domestic violence, or legalized gambling—still impact the larger society in which she lives. Discovering and analyzing the complexities of issues that encompass communal and societal realms as well as the world of personal experience is a valuable educational goal in the modern world.

Effectively addressing social problems requires familiarity with a constantly changing stream of data. Becoming well informed about today's controversies is an intricate process that often involves reading myriad primary and secondary sources, analyzing political debates, weighing various experts' opinions—even listening to firsthand accounts of those directly affected by the issue. For students and general observers, this can be a daunting task because of the sheer volume of information available in books, periodicals, on the evening news, and on the Internet. Researching the consequences of legalized gambling, for example, might entail sifting through congressional testimony on gambling's societal effects, examining private studies on Indian gaming, perusing numerous websites devoted to Internet betting, and reading essays written by lottery winners as well as interviews with recovering compulsive gamblers. Obtaining valuable information can be time-consuming—since it often requires researchers to pore over numerous documents and commentaries before discovering a source relevant to their particular investigation.

Greenhaven's Contemporary Issues Companion series seeks to assist this process of research by providing readers with useful and pertinent information about today's complex issues. Each volume in this anthology series focuses on a topic of current interest, presenting informative and thought-provoking selections written from a wide variety of viewpoints. The readings selected by the editors include such diverse sources as personal accounts and case studies, pertinent factual and statistical articles, and relevant commentaries and overviews. This diversity of sources and views, found in every Contemporary Issues Companion, offers readers a broad perspective in one convenient volume.

In addition, each title in the Contemporary Issues Companion series is designed especially for young adults. The selections included in every volume are chosen for their accessibility and are expertly edited in consideration of both the reading and comprehension levels of the audience. The structure of the anthologies also enhances accessibility. An introductory essay places each issue in context and provides helpful facts such as historical background or current statistics and legislation that pertain to the topic. The chapters that follow organize the material and focus on specific aspects of the book's topic. Every essay is introduced by a brief summary of its main points and biographical information about the author. These summaries aid in comprehension and can also serve to direct readers to material of immediate interest and need. Finally, a comprehensive index allows readers to efficiently scan and locate content.

The Contemporary Issues Companion series is an ideal launching point for research on a particular topic. Each anthology in the series is composed of readings taken from an extensive gamut of resources, including periodicals, newspapers, books, government documents, the publications of private and public organizations, and Internet websites. In these volumes, readers will find factual support suitable for use in reports, debates, speeches, and research papers. The anthologies also facilitate further research, featuring a book and periodical bibliography and a list of organizations to contact for additional information.

A perfect resource for both students and the general reader, Greenhaven's Contemporary Issues Companion series is sure to be a valued source of current, readable information on social problems that interest young adults. It is the editors' hope that readers will find the Contemporary Issues Companion series useful as a starting point to formulate their own opinions about and answers to the complex issues of the present day.

INTRODUCTION

Racetrack wagering is the unsung third component of legalized gambling in America. It is well overshadowed by the other members of the triad—casino gaming and state lotteries—because its revenues, though substantial, pale in comparison to casino and lottery revenues. In 2003, for example, commercial casinos raked in around $27 billion, while their cousins in the horse and dog racing industry brought in only about 10 percent of that amount. For this reason, economics professor Richard A. McGowan cites racetrack wagering in his book *Government and the Transformation of the Gaming Industry* as "a distant third" in the race to claim shares of U.S. legalized gambling revenues.

Though dog tracks contribute to overall revenues, the racing industry is led by the power and prestige of horse racing venues (thoroughbred and quarter horse tracks as well as harness racing circuits). Horse racing maintains its prestige because it retains the air of a sporting contest—the so-called sport of kings—and is not merely a means to wager money. While playing slot machines, for example, requires no skill, horse racing depends on the speed of the horses, the proficiency of the riders, and the wisdom of the gamblers. As McGowan writes, "Because of the skill involved in racing horses, horse-racing has always been able to soften any potential image problems caused by the close interaction between gambling and racing." In addition, McGowan claims that horse racing is simply a "mild release" for Americans who want to gamble. Therefore, state legislatures that harbor fears of what social ills might arise from tolerating "stronger" forms of legalized gambling, such as casinos, often condone horse racing. Having the approval of government and the support of a sports-enthused public allowed horse racing to keep its title as the "legitimate" form of gambling in America through the 1950s. Since that time, however, the racing industry has come to more closely follow the casino trend in America.

In the latter half of the twentieth century, the fortunes of the racing industry declined. The reinvention of state lotteries in the 1960s and the explosion of casino gambling in the 1990s were the undoing of horse racing's monopoly. Lotteries stole from horse racing the mild gamblers. Many such gamblers preferred to pick up a lottery ticket while shopping at a local mini-mart rather than spend all day at a track that was not within easy driving distance. Casinos, on the other hand, swallowed up the gamblers who desired the diversity of entertainments offered at a casino or were not satisfied with the slower pace of trackside wagering. Both lotteries and casinos also attracted larger gambling revenues because wagers could be made at any time of day, at any time of year—while respectable tracks were only open during specified hours in racing season. By the late 1990s the fate of racing seemed sealed. In their 2000 book *Jokers Wild: Legalized Gambling in the Twenty-first Century*, professors Thomas Barker and Marjie Britz assert, "The nation's racetracks are dying, victims of competition and other forms of gambling." Indeed, by then, many of America's racing venues had closed their doors.

The Racino Revolution

Many in the racetrack industry were not, however, willing to bow out gracefully to convenience gambling or fancy mega–resort-casinos. Industry leaders quickly recognized that to stay in competition, they had to cater to the changing wants of the American gambler. The first attempt was to embrace the electronic gaming market that had so long been the purview of casinos. In the late 1990s the AmTote Corporation created a computerized gambling machine that allowed players to wager on previously run races. The game, called Instant Racing, was tested at Oaklawn Park racetrack and the Southland Greyhound Park in West Memphis, Arkansas, in 2000. Instant Racing's video-game feel attracted a younger clientele, and revenues topped $5.8 million in 2004. Following Arkansas's success, two other states— Oregon and Wyoming—adopted Instant Racing, though Oregon relinquished its machines after a brief trial. While Instant Racing may not have been the salvation of the industry, its earnings proved that racetrack patrons had been influenced by the inundation of slot machines and video poker terminals during the 1990s casino boom and now wanted more instant gratification for their gambling dollars.

If the novelty of Instant Racing was not enough to compete with the banks of gleaming slot machines on a casino floor, many track operators concluded that the only way to survive—and keep the sport of horse racing alive—was to enter the casino market. Thus began the racino revolution. The industry looked to Mountaineer Park, a track in West Virginia that had added a hall of video poker terminals to its layout in 1990 and kept patronage high. The video poker machines are tied to the state lottery system and are technically referred to as video lottery terminals (VLTs). In 1992 Rhode Island's Lincoln Park dog track followed West Virginia's lead, and Delaware, Louisiana, and New York had installed banks of VLTs by 2004. In 1995 Iowa tried a different strategy and installed standard slot machines in one of its racetracks. New Mexico and the Delta Downs in Louisiana imitated this non-VLT model. Other states have since passed measures to allow racinos but have yet to open any.

The addition of slot machines and video poker terminals to veteran racetracks created unorthodox hybrids in the racing industry. Purists argued that the sport had been compromised, and pundits therefore coined the term *racino* to distinguish the unique crossbreed from traditional tracks. While some racing fans may have shied away from the bastardized tracks, racinos proved both popular and lucrative. According to gaming regulatory agencies in the six states that are home to racinos, gross revenues for 2003 topped $2.2 billion, and those earnings showed an increase of 10 percent from the previous year. To racino operators, the increased revenues are a blessing because they allow the tracks to run races with significantly higher purses, thus benefiting the jockeys and stables while at the same time attracting more patrons. The enormous earnings are also a welcome sight to state treasuries that either take a large slice via gambling taxes or profit directly through the money collected by the lottery-run VLTs.

The Impact of Racinos

Many state officials and legislators are understandably enticed by the earning power of racinos. In July 2004 Pennsylvania governor Ed Rendell won his campaign to vastly increase his state's tolerance of slot machines in order to lower property taxes. Using the popularity of Smarty Jones, a beloved horse that had nearly won the Triple Crown that year, the governor supported a bill that would add sixty-one thousand slot machines to seven Pennsylvania tracks (despite the fact that the state has only four tracks currently in operation). As reporter Jim Adams writes in *Indian Country Today*, the advent of so many slots in the northeast "is sure to speed up development of racinos in New York state and possibly to prod Maryland to end the impasse over its own slots legislation."

The racino domino effect recalls the casino boom of the 1990s, during which ten states pushed through commercial (non–Native American) casino legislation in order to keep their citizens' money from being lured into neighboring states that were either contemplating commercial casinos or already had Native American casinos in operation. That boom sharply divided communities and lawmakers over the moral, social, and economic impact of each new casino; many feared that the casinos would bring crime and promote the decay of established businesses that could not compete with the services offered by the casinos. In the new racino era, the same arguments are waged, but there is also a backlash coming from some sectors of the gambling industry as well. In Michigan, the state's casino operators are fighting plans to turn veteran tracks into racinos, fearing the loss of revenue to the competition. An April 2004 newswire reported that participants at an antiracino rally "warned that the racino bills would do significant economic harm to Detroit and Northern Michigan and every Michigan community that relies on casino gaming today for jobs, revenues and tourism."

Some complaints are also heard from Native American tribes that operate casinos in locations that are near proposed racinos. Many of the veteran gaming tribes, however, have opted to get in on the ground floor of the racino craze. The Connecticut Mashantucket who manage Foxwoods, the largest U.S. Indian casino, is but one of many tribes that are negotiating with track operators in hopes of bringing Native American casino expertise and money to the bargaining table. These tribes believe that existing racinos have made only a small dent in the drawing power of Native American casinos, making it far more logical to help create successful racinos from which all investing parties can reap the rewards.

Unfortunately for some segments of the racing industry, the resistance to racinos or the indecision of lawmakers still mulling over the legal ramifications have kept the racino boom from exploding in the way casinos did in the 1990s. This has meant that more and more tracks have folded operations because they have been unable to get the racino licensing they need in order to compete with nearby commercial and Native American casinos. In 2004 the harness track at Batavia Downs in upstate New York was such a victim. Although the state tolerates racinos, Batavia's poor financial health from years of lost revenue to nearby Native American casinos left it without the means to buy banks of VLTs—its proposed method of salvation. The track was forced to cancel its racing seasons indefinitely.

Current Trends and Future Predictions

With continuing declines in racetrack attendance and the closures of many venerable racing venues, the American racing industry retains only a small part of its former glory. Racing has not only been outpaced by the multibillion-dollar casino industry, it is being compelled to become part of the casino industry in order to survive. Indeed, the trend toward racinos is but one consequence of the larger trend in legalized gambling since the 1990s; that is, once casinos proved both lucrative and, at least, tolerable to a majority of Americans, their expansion dwarfed the competition and gobbled up the lion's share of the nation's gambling dollars. In addition to the drop in racetrack attendance, charitable gaming, card rooms, and bingo halls also felt a cut in revenues where casinos were within easy reach.

Survival strategies vary for each of these smaller gambling outlets, but many in the racing industry have come to the conclusion that if they cannot beat the competition, they are best advised to join it. Richard McGowan suspects that the holdouts to this policy will simply suffer bankruptcy. He predicts that soon "there will likely be a major consolidation of horse-racing tracks throughout the U.S., with 10 to 15 'supertracks' emerging as the only racing outlets." So far, this has yet to be racing's fate. As casino expansion is meeting more resistance from a public that is wearying of oversaturation, no one can foresee whether the marriage of casinos and the sport of kings will be the salvation of racing in America.

CHAPTER 1

AN OVERVIEW OF LEGALIZED GAMBLING IN AMERICA

A Short History of Gambling in the United States

Richard A. McGowan

Professor Richard A. McGowan provides the following brief history of gambling in America. McGowan describes the nation's five different "waves" of legalized gambling, from colonial days to the end of the twentieth century. Casino gambling remains the newest and dominant wave, he maintains, but state lotteries and pari-mutuel racetrack betting are still strong moneymakers. In addition, McGowan notes, the popularity of casino gaming and other legal forms of wagering reveals a national tolerance for gambling that will likely keep the industry alive and thriving in the twenty-first century. McGowan is an associate professor of the Carroll School of Management at Boston College and a research associate at Harvard Medical School's Division on Addictions. He researches business and public policy, especially as they relate to the gambling, tobacco, and alcohol industries. He is also the author of *State Lotteries and Legalized Gambling: Painless Revenue or Painful Mirage* and *Government and the Transformation of the Gaming Industry*, from which this selection is taken.

In 1984, all forms of gambling (casinos, lotteries, *pari-mutuel* betting: the three segments of the gambling industry) accounted for less than $15 billion in revenues. In 1995, these gambling activities generated $55.3 billion in revenues, nearly a 400 per cent increase in 11 years. Gambling had become the largest component of the American entertainment industry. It had also become a means of salvation in terms of economic development for troubled urban areas ranging from Chicago to New Bedford, Massachusetts. But the multiple roles that gambling presently fulfils, namely a form of entertainment, a method of raising revenue for states and a measure that would provide economic relief for depressed areas, are hardly unique in American history.

There have been five waves of gambling activity that have occurred in US history. . . .

State-Sanctioned Lotteries

The first wave of gaming activity (1607–1840s) that occurred in the US began with the landing of the first settlers, but became much more widespread with the outbreak of the Revolutionary War. During this time, lotteries were the approved form of gambling. A few of these lotteries were sponsored by states to help finance their armies, but most lotteries were operated by non-profit making institutions such as colleges, local school systems and hospitals in order to finance building projects or needed capital improvements. For example, both Yale and Harvard . . . used lotteries to build their dormitories. In 1747, the Connecticut legislature gave Yale a license to raise £7,500 while Harvard waited until 1765 to win approval from the Massachusetts' legislature to conduct a lottery worth £3,200. It is interesting to note that Harvard's fund-raising lottery was much less successful than Yale's lottery. The primary reason for the failure of Harvard's lottery was that it had to compete with lotteries that were being operated to support troops which were fighting the French and Indian War. However, it certainly appears that Harvard has learned from its past mistakes, as the timing of its fund-raising activities has greatly improved! It should also be noted that during this wave of lottery activity, no state ever operated its own lottery. Private operators conducted lotteries. An organization or a worthy project such as the Erie Canal received permission from state legislatures to operate a lottery. The funds from the lottery were used to support the 'worthy' cause.

But these private operators of lotteries often proved to be less than honest in conducting these lotteries. One of the more famous lottery scandals occurred in Washington, DC. In 1823, Congress authorized a Grand National lottery in order to pay for improvements to the city. Tickets were sold and the drawing took place, but before anyone could collect their winnings, the private agent who organized the lottery for DC fled town. While the majority of winners accepted their fate with resignation, the winner of the $100,000 grand prize sued the government of District of Columbia and the Supreme Court ruled that DC had to pay the winner. It was a sober reminder to local officials that authorizing lotteries could be potentially dangerous, and the movement to ban lotteries had begun. From 1840 to 1860, all but two states prohibited lottery activity due to various scandals that occurred in the 1820s and 1830s. However, it would take less than 40 years for lotteries to once again explode on the national scene.

National Lotteries

With the conclusion of the Civil War, the South had to find some method to finance the construction of roads, bridges, school buildings and various other social capital projects due to the damage incurred during the Civil War. The victorious North was in no mood to provide for its defeated cousins, hence southern legislatures were desperate to raise revenues. One way to raise these sorely needed funds was to permit private operators to conduct lotteries in order to raise the revenue needed for reconstruction. The primary difference between this period of lottery activity and the previous period of lotteries is the scale of ticket sales. Whereas in the previous lottery boom sales of tickets were confined to local regions, these southern lotteries took on a national scope and ironically were particularly popular in the North. The most famous of these southern lotteries was the one conducted in Louisiana known as the Serpent. At the height of this lottery in the late 1880s, almost 50 per cent of all mail coming into New Orleans was connected with this lottery.

As was the case with the first wave of lottery activity, controversy surrounded this national lottery activity that eventually led to its banning by the Federal government. In 1890, the charter that authorized the running of the lottery in Louisiana was about to expire. The operators of the lottery bribed various state officials with offers of up to $100,000 to renew the Serpent's charter. The rather flagrant method that officials of the lottery employed to ensure that the Serpent's charter would be renewed was reported throughout the country. Various state legislatures passed resolutions calling on Congress and President [William Henry] Harrison to stop this lottery. There can be little doubt that what upset these legislatures most was the fact that out-of-states sales of Louisiana lottery tickets amounted to over $5 million per year. President Harrison urged Congress to pass legislation to curb all lottery activity. The primary piece of legislation that would cripple the Louisiana lottery was to deny the operators of the lottery the use of the federal mail. If customers could no longer mail in their requests for tickets, then the lottery's life would be short-lived. In late 1890, Congress banned the use of federal mails for lottery sales. By 1895, the Louisiana lottery had vanished and as the new century dawned, gaming activity in the US had ceased to exist. But, like a phoenix, lotteries as well as other forms of gaming would again be resurrected as governments searched for additional sources of revenue in the late twentieth century.

The Golden Age of *Pari-Mutuel* Betting

In the midst of the Prohibition era, a quiet revolution involving another 'sin' industry, gambling, was taking place. The two states, Kentucky and Maryland, which had the longest tradition of horse racing, decided to legalize wagering on horse races taking place in racetracks that had long and noble histories. Kentucky and Maryland sanctioned *pari-mutuel* betting for two reasons. First, these states were searching for a means to replace the excise tax revenues that were lost due to the imposition of Prohibition by the Federal government. Second, technology had been developed that permitted the advent of the *pari-mutuel* betting system, where the winners divide the total amount bet, after deducting management's expenses and state's taxes, in proportion to the sums that have been wagered individually. With the start of the Great Depression in 1929, numerous other states were also seeking any source of additional revenue. They were quick to follow the lead of Kentucky and Maryland in enacting legalized *pari-mutuel* betting. Since the 1920s, 45 states have legalized *pari-mutuel* betting with Alabama, Mississippi, Missouri, North Carolina and South Carolina being the last 'holdouts'. However . . . , both Mississippi and Missouri have jumped on the gambling bandwagon in other ways.

What enabled these states to 'legitimize' *pari-mutuel* betting so easily and rapidly, especially during a time when another 'sin', alcohol, had been totally banned? Traditionally, racing—particularly horse racing—has sold itself as a sport, softening potential image problems caused by its association with gambling. Horse racing and other forms of racing, such as dog racing, are covered in the sports pages of most major newspapers and the 'superstars' of horse racing have appeared on the front cover of *Time* and *Sports Illustrated*. Racetracks such as Churchill Downs in Kentucky and Saratoga in upstate New York also emphasize the traditional pageantry associated with racing, such as parading the horses in the paddock, trumpeting the call to post and so on. Another factor that contributed to the 'legitimacy' of racing was that 'honesty' was assured, since some of America's wealthiest families such as the Vanderbilts, the Whitneys, and the Rockefellers controlled the racing industry. All of these factors not only contributed to the legitimacy of racing, but have also made horse racing one of the biggest sports throughout the period from 1920 to 1960.

It also gave *pari-mutuel* betting a virtual monopoly on gambling activity in the US throughout the middle period of the twentieth century. The racing industry's only competition was in Nevada, that had legalized casino gambling in 1930.

State-Operated Lotteries

In 1964, New Hampshire voters approved the lottery, a form of gambling that had been utilized earlier in US history. The rationale used by proponents of the lottery to justify its legalization was strictly economic. Proceeds from the lottery were to fund education, thereby averting the enactment of either a sales or income tax for New Hampshire. The lottery was an instant success with 90 per cent of the lottery tickets being bought by out of state residents.

But this lesson was not lost on neighbouring north-eastern states. In the next ten years, every north-eastern state approved a lottery. Two rationales were used to justify the lottery activity in all these states:

1. People are going to gamble, so why shouldn't the state profit from this activity;
2. Neighbouring states were reaping benefits from constituents buy-

ing lottery tickets in those states, therefore the state needed to institute a lottery in order to keep the money 'home'.

One of the more interesting aspects of this surge of lottery activity is that these lotteries were operated by state agencies. They were not only state-sanctioned, but also operated by state governments.

However, the greatest growth of state lotteries occurred in the period between 1980 and 1990. During this time, 25 states not only approved lotteries but other additional forms of gambling such as off-track betting (OTB), keno (a type of high stakes bingo that is played every five minutes) and video poker machines (usually found in bars and restaurants). All of these new forms were meant to supplement the revenue capabilities of lotteries. By 1993, only two states (Utah and Hawaii) did not have some form of legalized gaming. Lotteries and associated forms of gaming had gained a social acceptance that had not occurred in previous waves of lottery activity. . . .

The Triumph of Casino Gaming

In 1993, for the first time in US gaming history, revenues for casino gaming were greater than those generated by lotteries. This occurrence heralded a remarkable turning point for the gambling industry. Casino gambling was now the preferred form of gaming in the US. It also marks a turning point on American acceptance of gambling as a legal source of entertainment. Finally, this development returns the control of gambling operations to private concerns, since the casino gaming operations are owned and operated by private corporations although they are certainly heavily regulated by the states. . . .

How did this expansion of casino gaming take place? There is a three-part explanation for this rise in casino gaming. First, during the late 1980s, the two 'traditional' markets for casino gambling, Las Vegas and Atlantic City, transformed themselves from strictly casino operations to 'family' oriented vacation centers. For example, in trying to renew its Las Vegas operations, MGM not only renovated its casino operation but also built a theme park. In Atlantic City, casino operators were able to add hotel rooms as well as receiving relief from various regulations concerning their operations. The threat that Native American Gambling . . . posed persuaded New Jersey legislators to protect its casino industry. Overall, these two locations experienced a 22 per cent increase in gaming revenues and a 24 per cent increase in visitors during the early 1990s.

The other form of casino gambling that became popular in the 1990s was riverboat gambling. In 1989, Iowa was the first state to permit it, soon to be followed by Louisiana, Illinois, Indiana, Mississippi and Missouri. It is interesting to note that all of these states had lotteries except for Mississippi. Why this turn to riverboat gambling? Riverboat gambling was portrayed as a limited form of casino gambling. Players could only play for two hours at a time and for only a set amount of money. For example, in 1990, when Iowa established its riverboat gambling, the boats had to sail for two hours and patrons were only permitted to bring $500. After the boat docked, all the patrons had to leave the boat and new patrons were permitted to board for another cruise. Yet, as other states entered the riverboat gambling industry, these restrictions were gradually lifted so that virtually no restrictions remain.

The final source of casino revenues is the Indian casino gaming operations. In 1988, Congress passed the Indian Gaming Regulatory Act (IGRA) that permitted Indian tribes to develop casino and bingo parlors into major economic centers. By far the most successful of these Indian casinos has been Foxwoods in Connecticut, which is the world's largest casino generating nearly $800 million in 1995. Revenues from Indian casino operations exceeded lottery revenues in 1995. . . .

Casino gambling has clearly become the dominant force behind a virtual explosion of gambling activity in the US. Clearly gambling, and in particular casino gambling, has become socially acceptable. . . . Throughout the 1990s between 85 per cent to 90 per cent of the US adult population believed that gambling was an acceptable form of entertainment, while between 10 per cent to 15 per cent of the US adult population thought that it was an activity that government ought to outlaw or prohibit. Gambling had achieved 'legitimacy' as an activity and was now 'tolerated' by government because it was seen as a source of revenue and an engine of economic renewal for depressed areas.

THE RISE OF NATIVE AMERICAN GAMING

William N. Thompson

William N. Thompson, professor of public administration at the University of Nevada, Las Vegas, is a noted authority on gambling in America and has written several books on the subject. In the following selection Thompson traces the history of Native American gaming, from its roots in high-stakes bingo to the rise of Las Vegas–style resort casinos on tribal land. According to Thompson, the explosive growth of Indian gaming in the 1990s was sparked by the passage of the 1988 Indian Gaming Regulatory Act, a federal law that preserved the right of Native American tribes to establish and operate gaming enterprises without significant state or federal intervention. Since the passage of the act, he explains, the relationship between gaming tribes and their state governments has often been strained.

Although Native Americans had traditionally participated in various kinds of games that included prizes and could be considered gambling activities, commercial gaming operations were not found on reservations until very recently. Not unrelated is that very few commercial gambling operations were anywhere until very recently. However, with the restoration of government-sponsored lotteries in the 1960s, the public began to demand the operation of games to benefit charities of one kind or another. Soon many states were permitting churches and other nonprofit groups to conduct bingo and other lower-stakes games to raise revenues.

High-Stakes Bingo

In the 1970s, many Native American tribes began to participate in charity gaming in accordance with state rules regarding how the games would be played and the types of prizes that could be offered. Then, in 1978, the Florida Seminole Nation decided to do things differently at their bingo hall. Faced with competition from other charities, they threw aside the state's prize limits and began a high-stakes

William N. Thompson, "History, Development, and Legislation of Native American Casino Gaming," in *Legalized Casino Gaming in the United States: The Economic and Social Impact*, ed. Cathy H.C. Hsu. Binghamton, NY: The Haworth Hospitality Press, an imprint of The Haworth Press, Inc., 1999. Copyright © 1999 by The Haworth Press, Inc. All rights reserved. Reproduced by permission.

game with prizes in the tens of thousands of dollars. Players flocked to the Miami suburb of Hollywood where the Seminole bingo hall was located. Rival bingo games run by charitable groups took a major hit. Their sponsors were not amused.

Nor were state and local government officials. The Broward County sheriff, Robert Butterworth, filed criminal charges and sought to close down the Seminole bingo game. His actions led to a series of law cases, culminating in the 1981 approval of games without state limits by a federal court of appeals (*Seminole Tribe of Florida v. Butterworth*, 1981). In 1982, the U.S. Supreme Court refused to review the ruling (*Seminole Tribe of Florida v. Butterworth*, 1982). Key to the case was that in Florida, bingo was legal and could be played. The tribes were only violating the manner in which the games were played.

Tribes across the United States took notice of the gaming activities and especially of legal cases that affirmed the special status tribes enjoyed in this realm of economic enterprise. Gaming began to appear on most of the reservations in America. However, except for internal tribal regulations, there was almost no supervision of the gaming activities. And the activities involved large sums of money.

The Regulation Debate

Problems arise when there is little independent regulation of large-scale gaming. In regard to Native American bingo games, some cases revealed that non-Indian managers were setting up games and taking the bulk of the revenues. Members of organized crime families made their presence felt on some reservations. Also, some unscrupulous tribal members used gaming for personal advantages in ways adverse to their tribe's interests. As the 1980s progressed, the need for independent oversight of Native American gaming was recognized. Congress began to explore the manner in which the gaming could be regulated. The first bills to regulate tribal gaming were introduced in 1984. Hearings were held over the next three years; however, no consensus developed over the manner of regulation that should be set into place. State governments wanted federal authorization for them to oversee the regulation or, alternatively, to have federal regulations that incorporated all the state rules on non-native gaming. The tribes opposed the notion of any state control over their gaming. An impasse ensued.

The impasse could not be resolved easily because during this same time, a case [*California v. Cabazon Band of Mission Indians*] was wending its way to the U.S. Supreme Court. The case essentially was designed to gain a review of the earlier Florida case. State interests were optimistic that the Court would overturn the earlier ruling and allow state rules on gaming to apply to the tribes. They were not about to make any compromises in Congress while the case was pending. The tribes, on the other hand, were leaning toward concessions that would allow some federal regulation.

The political formula changed when, in February 1987, the Court ruled in a 6-3 vote that the earlier decisions would stand—that states could not impose their civil regulations on Native American gaming operations. Moreover, the Court endorsed gaming as being consistent with federal policies designed to promote self-sufficiency for tribes. . . . The Court added, "self-determination and economic development are not within reach if the Tribes cannot raise revenues and provide employment for their members. The Tribes' interests obviously parallel the federal interests" (*California v. Cabazon Band of Mission Indians,* 1987). The Court added that regulation by any nontribal entity could take place only if a specific act of Congress called for such measures. The states besieged members of Congress to act. Tribal interests were less inclined to endorse congressional action, as the status quo was quite acceptable to them. However, they agreed to a compromise. The Indian Gaming Regulatory Act (IGRA) was passed and signed into law by President [Ronald] Reagan on October 7, 1988 (IGRA, 1988).

Two tribes, the Minnesota Red Lake Band of Chippewa and the Mescalero Apache Tribe of New Mexico, immediately challenged the constitutionality of the act, claiming that it was an infringement upon their sovereignty. However, federal courts denied their claim, and the Supreme Court refused to hear their appeal (*Red Lake Band v. Swimmer,* 1990). That was not the end to constitutional challenges to the act, however.

An Overview of the IGRA

Congress identified the purpose of the act as establishing a "statutory basis for the operation of gaming by Indian tribes as a means of promoting tribal economic development, self-sufficiency, and strong tribal governments." Congress further recognized the need to shield tribal interests from organized crime and to ensure that tribal members received the gaming revenues.

The IGRA established a three-member National Indian Gaming Commission. Two of the members were Native Americans. The commission was empowered to regulate bingo-type games on reservations and to promulgate general rules for Native American gaming pertaining to contracts with outside companies. Casino-type gaming was to be regulated in accordance with rules established in negotiations between the tribes and the state governments. If the states refused to negotiate in good faith, they could be mandated to do so by federal courts.

Starting in 1989, many court mandates prompted states to enter into negotiations allowing casino gaming on reservations. However, on March 27, 1996, in a 5-4 vote, the U.S. Supreme Court ruled that the provision of the act which allowed tribes to sue states in federal courts over the lack of good faith negotiations was unconstitutional because of the Eleventh Amendment. The amendment implies that states are sovereign units and cannot be sued in federal courts except by other states, foreign countries, or the federal government.

The Court did not rule the entire act unconstitutional, nor did the Court address how negotiation impasses would be resolved in the future—whether states could simply say "no" to tribes, or whether tribes could go to the secretary of the interior for relief.

Classes of Gaming

The IGRA delineated three classes of gaming. Class I gaming consists of small prize games between tribal members. It also consists of games traditionally played by tribes in ceremonies or celebrations. These activities are regulated entirely by the tribes. No issues have arisen over Class I games since the passage of the act.

Class II gaming encompasses bingo in its various forms, as well as pull-tab cards, punch boards, and tip jars,[1] Certain card games such as poker also are included as long as the games are nonbanking, that is, do not involve bets between the casino and the player, rather only bets among players.

In four specific states—Michigan, North Dakota, South Dakota, and Washington—banked card games, specifically blackjack games, were to be regulated as Class II games if the games were played in the tribal casinos before the act passed. Elsewhere, blackjack and other banked card games were to be regulated as Class III games.

Tribes can conduct Class II gaming as long as the game involved is permitted in the state to be played "for any purpose, by any person, organization or entity." The tribe must first pass an ordinance to offer Class II games. The ordinance must be approved by the commission chairman, and the commission then conducts background investigations on the gaming facility and its employees.

The commission regulates the gaming for a period of three years, after which the tribe can apply for permission to self-regulate the Class II games. Most tribes have successfully won permission for self-regulation. The permission can be revoked if the commission believes that the self-regulation efforts are inadequate. While the commission regulates the gaming, it may assess the tribes a fee for the cost involved.

Class III gaming consists of all forms of gaming not covered by Class I and Class II definitions. Basically, the Class III category covers all casino-banked games, including blackjack, baccarat, roulette, craps, and all slot machines. Class III also includes lottery games as conducted by state governments and pari-mutuel racing wagers. As with Class II games, the Class III games may be played only if the tribe has an ordinance permitting them and if the games are permitted "for any purpose, by any person, organization or entity" in the state where the tribal facility is located.

1. These games, like bingo, are played in one location and guarantee at least one winner.

Also, for Class III gaming to be permitted, the tribe must enter into a compact with the state. The compact will provide a detailed provision on games allowed in the facility, the manner of offering the games, and the regulatory structures for oversight of the games. If a state refused to enter into negotiations in good faith for Class III games, the tribe was authorized to seek federal court mandates for negotiations. After the mandates were issued, if the state continued to refuse to negotiate, the court could appoint a mediator, who would be empowered to select a proposed compact offered by either the tribe or the state. The secretary of the interior would then certify the compact as being in force.

The complications placed upon the process by the Supreme Court's ruling that the tribes could not seek relief in federal courts if the states refused to negotiate in good faith linger. [Former] Secretary of the Interior Bruce Babbitt . . . sought comments on a procedure that would allow the tribes and states to directly present their proposed compacts to the secretary's office for approval, in effect, bypassing the court process altogether. Such a procedure may be attempted in the near future,[2] but the concern is whether the secretary would or legally could force a compact upon an unwilling participant in the process—be that a tribe or state.

Enforcement, Taxation, and Revenues

The Class III compacts may provide very specific authority for tribal and nontribal (whether county, city, or state) law enforcement agencies to supervise and enforce provisions of the gaming agreements. Without such authority, all enforcement activities regarding gaming on Indian lands remains in the hands of the tribal government and the federal government. In other words, without a compact, even if tribes are permitting games the state believes to be Class III games, the state cannot enforce the law. The state must wait for federal district attorneys and marshals to make all enforcement actions. State governments may not tax the native gaming facilities. However, as with the federal government, the state may charge the tribes sums of money to cover the actual costs of state regulation of the facilities.

The tribe's share of net revenues must go for tribal purposes. If the tribe shows that it is meeting its obligations to provide for the social welfare of its members, it may authorize up to 40 percent to go to individual members in a per capita distribution. One small Minnesota tribe has given its members as much as $700,000 each as their annual share of gaming proceeds. . . .

2. Babbitt adopted new rules in 1999 over objections that he had exceeded his authority. Gale Norton, who took the office of interior secretary in 2001, has enforced the Babbitt rules. Lawsuits against the secretary for exceeding her authority are pending.

The most successful Native American casino [Foxwoods] is in Led-yard, Connecticut. Governor Lowell Weicker had refused to negotiate agreements, claiming casino games were illegal in the state. However, the state did permit table games for charities on special "Las Vegas Nights." The tribe won a court mandate ordering the governor to ne-gotiate. He refused. A mediator was appointed. The tribe and gover-nor both submitted proposed compacts. The governor's proposal actu-ally included provisions for allowing table games. The mediator selected the governor's proposal. Then the state appealed the selec-tion, asking the secretary of the interior to reject its own proposal. The secretary of the interior instead signed the proposal, and it be-came the compact (*Mashantucket Pequot v. Connecticut,* 1990).

Clearly, the state of Connecticut did not permit anyone to have slot machines. Also, the IGRA clearly says states cannot tax tribal gaming. Nonetheless, in 1993, the state and its governor reached a "side agreement" with the tribes to allow them to have as many slot machines as they wanted, providing they paid the state 25 percent of the revenue from the machines. The agreement was never approved by the secretary of the interior (how could it be, since it was patently illegal?), but the casino offers slot machines—5,500 of them—for its customers. The 25 percent tax was called a monopoly fee. It would go to the state only as long as the Mashantucket Pequots had a monop-oly on the machines (how could they possibly be permitted to others under the circumstances?). The monopoly ended in 1996 when a sec-ond tribe opened a casino, and the 25 percent share was renegotiated with the governor's office, without the approval of federal authorities. The state of Connecticut received approximately $160 million a year as its share of the slot revenues.

In Minnesota, Governor Arne Carlson refused to negotiate an agreement for table games. However, the tribe persuaded the federal court authorities that a law allowing social gaming in homes among friends constituted permitted gaming. When ordered to negotiate, the governor signed an agreement allowing blackjack in tribal casinos. Next, they asked for slot machines on the basis that recreational slots were in taverns and winners could win free games. The governor signed an agreement to allow video gaming machines.

In Wisconsin, a strange series of events found tribes and Governor Tommy Thompson at an impasse. Federal Judge Barbara Crabb ordered that the state allow the tribes to have casinos. No one else in the state was permitted to have any casino games. However, in the past, casino gaming had been outlawed on the basis of a state constitutional provi-sion banning lotteries. But in April 1987, state voters removed the con-stitutional ban. The legislature then created a state lottery authority and authorized it to offer games of consideration, chance, and prize—a general definition that covers almost all casino games. The lottery only offered regular lottery-type games, but Judge Crabb ruled that the statute was written to permit casino games if the lottery desired to have them (*Lac du Flambeau Band v. Wisconsin,* 1991).

She ordered the governor to negotiate an agreement allowing casino games. He promptly appealed the decision. Almost as promptly, he offered to let the tribes have machines and blackjack as the Minnesota casinos had. The 1993 compacts had a five-year limit. Most of the tribes agreed, and casinos began in earnest on the Wisconsin reservation. . . .

Here to Stay

Many questions remain, making the policy arena for Native American gambling a puzzling one. A new factor has come into the process since it first began. Many Native American tribes are now very powerful players in the political process. The Mashantucket Pequots have a very active lobbying force in Washington, DC. They gave considerable amounts to many political candidates in both parties. They were among the leading three contributors to President [Bill] Clinton's re-election campaign. The Sault St. Marie tribe in Michigan was the leading contributor in state elections in 1996. This new power arises out of tribal resources gained from gaming operations. The money is focused upon policymakers who have to consider questions involving Native American gaming. It can be safely concluded that Native American gaming is here to stay for quite a while.

THE DEVELOPMENT OF STATE-RUN LOTTERIES

Thomas Barker and Marjie Britz

Lotteries have been part of American history since colonial days. Early lotteries were used to raise money to build public projects and fund charitable causes. Modern lotteries, though, have little in common with their predecessors. As Thomas Barker and Marjie Britz assert in the following article, contemporary state-run lotteries are a means to increase state budgets. Following a period of prohibition, states turned to lotteries in the 1960s as a way to increase revenues without raising taxes. Since that time, Barker and Britz note, state lotteries have evolved into a multibillion-dollar industry. However, in reinstating lotteries, the authors argue, the states have embraced the ethically questionable position of promoting gambling—a vice that otherwise is held in check by government regulation.

Thomas Barker is a professor of criminal justice and police studies at Eastern Kentucky University. He has written several books on criminal justice and researched gambling for more than thirty years. Marjie Britz is a professor in the political science department of The Citadel in South Carolina. She has written mainly on issues of criminal justice.

The modern state-run lotteries are different in many ways from earlier chance drawings, even from the public lotteries that were a part of our nation's history. . . . The modern-day state lottery is first and foremost a gambling lottery, not "choosing by lots" to fairly distribute (by chance) good or bad things. . . . Choosing by lots occurs in sports drafts and injury selection, and in previous years, it has been used to determine selection for military service (World War II and Vietnam in the later years). However, these drawings by chance are not gambling-lotteries. Gambling-lotteries, unlike choosing by lots, involve chance, consideration (something of value), and a prize/reward. The player purchases a chance to win a prize, based on a random drawing. Lotteries are considered different from other forms of gambling because the outcome of the game is determined solely by chance, with no skill involved.

State-Run Monopolies

Gambling-lotteries are state-run monopolies staffed by career-minded bureaucrats, often more interested in revenue generation than the player's welfare or benefit. The modern lotteries are political creations, and their mandates, goals, and revenue potentials change with each session of the legislature and new administration, Lottery directors in states where the lotteries are viewed as "cash cows" feeding into the state's general fund sometimes find themselves under pressure from politicians to increase profits by introducing new games or lowering the payback. State-run lotteries, particularly three- and four-number picks, are the movement of the "numbers racket" [an illegal daily lottery] from the neighborhoods to the state capitals, often with less favorable odds, convenience, and payout. The state-run "brass ring" confuses the state's proper role in public policy and gambling. The state in initiating a gambling-lottery moves from the prohibition of gambling-lotteries—Thou Shalt Not—to permission—You May—to promotion—Please Do. . . .

[Thirty-eight] states, including Washington, D.C., have gambling-lotteries. The lottery is also a worldwide form of gambling—100 countries. The games played in the U.S. gambling-lotteries include instant and pull-tabs, lotto, three- and four-number daily games, five number games, multistate Powerball (21 states), and Big Game (6 states) lottos, keno, and video lottery terminals [VLTs]. . . .

From the players' standpoint, VLTs, often referred to as the "crack cocaine of gambling," have the lowest payback percentage. Slot machines are the most profitable games in casinos. VLTs are the most profitable lottery games. In 1997, Delaware's VLTs revenue accounted for 83.8 percent of the lottery revenue. West Virginia's VLTs accounted for 54.1 percent of the state's lottery revenues and South Dakota's VLTs were the largest source of lottery revenues. Nationwide, 44.9 cents of every dollar spent on lottery tickets is returned to the players. However . . . , this varies by state. Governments retained as revenues 32 cents of every dollar bet. International Gaming & Wagering Business (IGWB) states, "Casinos and racetracks make greater contributions to employment, but in terms of direct contributions to government budgets, lotteries stand alone." . . .

New Hampshire Begins the New Craze

Casino gambling had been legalized in Nevada (1931) and 26 states had legalized horse racing by 1963. Gallup polls from 1941 to 1963 revealed that popular support for government lotteries was strong and growing. In fact, there was a general softening of public opinion toward all forms of gambling. However, lotteries were prohibited by all the states. The policy was Thou Shall Not. This changed with the New Hampshire Lottery.

The New Hampshire legislature prior to 1963 had considered lottery bills, one passed in 1955, but it was vetoed by the governor. However, in 1963 New Hampshire, without a sales or income tax, needed additional revenues for public services, particularly education, then ranked lowest in the nation in state aid. Pro-lottery forces pointed out that a state-run lottery could provide revenues and support education without resorting to new taxes. Then, as now, the principal selling point for state-run lotteries was revenue generation. Revenue is the raison d'être of state lotteries. A "painless" means to raise public revenues without increasing taxes. The bill was passed by the legislature, signed by the governor, and approved in a 1964 statewide referendum.

The first lottery in the twentieth century was primitive when compared to the modern multimillion-dollar lotteries of today. The 1964 New Hampshire Lottery resembled the early colonial sweepstakes/lotteries: Winning tickets were drawn from a pool of tickets purchased, originally twice a year. Like the common church, school, and civic group raffles of today, a purchaser wrote his or her name and address on one side of a ticket and held the stub until the drawing. The winning ticket was chosen from among all the tickets sold. The $3 tickets were purchased from state agents at racetracks and state-liquor stores. New Hampshire returned 31 cents of every dollar bet back to the players. The New Hampshire Lottery was an instant success—$58.6 million in sales the first year, largely due to the influx of out-of-state ticket buyers. However, it went into a five-year ticket sales decline. In 1968 the lottery was running a poor second to horse racing in terms of money wagered. The passive nature of the lottery was the prime reason for its decline. Lottery players did not "play" the game as in horse racing, and they had to wait a long time to find out if they won.

New York and New Jersey Innovations

New York, seeing the success of the New Hampshire Lottery, began operating a lottery in 1967. The number of New York residents playing the nearby New Hampshire Lottery was also a big factor in the lottery's passage in the New York legislature. Lotteries are an example of . . . the domino effect. Neighboring states pass lotteries to keep their citizens' money at home. In order to compete against New Hampshire, New York increased drawings to once a month but also required players to write their names and addresses on the ticket. New York's $1 lottery tickets were sold at banks and certain public offices. The payout was set at 40 cents per dollar bet, 9 cents higher than New Hampshire. A portion of the lottery revenues was designated as supplemental aid to public schools. . . .

The success of state lotteries as "money" machines came with New

Jersey's introduction of computer-numbered tickets, 50-cent tickets, weekly drawings, and modern marketing techniques. The New Jersey legislature designated the lottery net proceeds (after prizes and expenses) to be used for state institutions and state aid for education, including higher education and senior citizen education. New Jersey's lottery was an instant success ($1.1 billion), and its revenues did not decline as they had in New Hampshire and New York.

Lotto and Instant Tickets

Prior to the lotto, preprinted lottery tickets were matched to the numbers drawn. New York's lotto game allowed players to pick their own numbers from a selected field (6 out of a field of 42) through networks of computer terminals at retail outlets. Lotto allowed for the player's active involvement in the game (choosing the numbers). Even more significant to the lotto's appeal was that it allowed jackpots to "roll over" until a player/s won. In effect, lotto is a parimutuel game, with the jackpot set equal to a percentage of the amount bet. This amount varies by state. If there is no jackpot winner in a drawing, the set percentage "rolls" over to the next drawing.

Following New York's lead, New Jersey began using the lotto in 1980, with other lottery states soon making the switch. These states used a form of the lotto with the field of numbers to choose from ranging from 30 to 50. The larger the field, the more combinations of numbers to choose and an increased likelihood of a rollover. The lotto is a game of long odds and huge jackpots. . . . The rollover feature of the lotto, and its potential to produce large jackpots, is the one characteristic that sets the lotto apart from all other lottery games. It is strictly a "going for the dream" game.

The development and introduction of the world's first "secure" instant tickets, "paper slot machines," by Scientific Games International (SGI) (headquarters in Alpharetta, Georgia), was the next lottery innovation. The instant ticket first used in Massachusetts in 1974 allowed the player to know immediately whether or not he or she had won a prize. Tickets were winners if they matched a combination of numbers, letters, or words hidden under a vinyl cover the player scratched off. The instant tickets developed by Scientific Games made it impossible to counterfeit tickets, see through the rub-off layer, or alter the tickets once sold. By 1982 all state lotteries were using some form of instant game.

Instant games have been useful for states in the start-up phase of their lotteries. Scratch-offs can be easily distributed to retailers, and they are quick and easy to play. Instant tickets are the most cost-effective means of establishing a retailer network and player base. States often begin their lotteries with the sale of instant tickets until they raise enough revenue to set up the interconnected computer terminals for the sale of lottery tickets. The South Dakota (1987) Lottery repaid the $1.5 million start-up loan plus interest to the state in three months by selling instant tickets. Florida repaid its $15.5 million start-up loan plus interest to the General Revenue Fund 17 days after it began the sale of instant tickets. . . .

Pick 3 and Pick 4

[Gambling critics and lottery historians Charles T.] Clotfelter and [Philip J.] Cook call the state lotteries' Pick 3 and 4 numbers game the "Sincerest Form of Flattery" to the illegal numbers game run by organized crime. That statement is not too far from the truth. The legal and illegal numbers games share a number of common characteristics. Furthermore, when the New Jersey legislators instituted the Pick 3 numbers game [in 1975], they thought they would drive the illegal games out of business.

The illegal numbers games that became popular in the Northeast during the 1920s were based on simple three-digit number selection, usually the last three numbers in the handle from local racetracks. The bettor could choose a straight bet, all three numbers in exact order; a boxed bet, six combinations of the three numbers; a single bet, one of the numbers; or two digits. The bets could be for as low as a nickel and often on credit. The collectors sold door to door, in stores and newsstands, or by phone. Typically, the bet was payed off at 500 or 600 to 1. The true odds were 1,000 to 1.

The legal numbers games offer no credit and allow no bet less than 50 cents. Straight bets and boxed bets are allowed but not single- or two-number bets; however, Florida and Missouri allow players to choose the first two or the last two digits of their CA$H 3. Payoff odds are 500 to 1. Numbers are randomly drawn from the field 0 through 9, with replacement, by the lottery commission, usually on a daily basis. Trust in the random selection by the state and the instant publication of results—TV and radio—have led the illegal numbers games to use the same numbers. The first televised lottery drawing was in 1977 (Delaware).

The legal numbers games have not appeared to impact the illegal games that operated before the state lotteries instituted the numbers game. The illegal games are still more convenient to the players and offer credit, a smaller minimum bet, and no payment of taxes. Often, the payouts are higher than the legal games. Nevertheless, Pick 3 and 4 numbers games are popular and profitable for the states.

Entertainment and Convenience

State lotteries since their legalization in 1964 have come a long way. Today lotteries are much more than players risking a small amount against long odds to win a big prize. The innovations of lotto, instant games, and numbers have made the modern state-run lotteries quite different from earlier lotteries. State-run gambling lotteries are a major part of the U.S. gambling industry. The lotteries, like the "gaming" industry, claim they are part of the entertainment industry: One of the Michigan Lottery's missions is to: "Provide quality entertainment to the public." The mission of the Missouri Lottery is "to maximize revenues for public education through the creation and sales of fun and entertaining products." Georgia seeks "[t]o maximize revenues for specific education programs by providing entertaining lottery products." Nebraska states that "players and winners alike enjoy the high quality entertainment option provided by Nebraska scratch games and lotto games."

Lotteries are the most popular (based on participation) and widely and conveniently available form of legalized gambling in the United States. . . . Lottery retailers have a vested interest in lottery sales. In Missouri, retailers receive 2 percent of all online redemptions and 2 percent of all cash redemptions on instant tickets. They also receive $50,000 for selling a Powerball jackpot ticket and 1 percent of a Missouri Lotto jackpot prize for selling the winning ticket. In South Dakota, instant ticket retailers are paid a 5 percent commission. They also receive a 1 percent bonus on all prizes over $100 sold in their stores and a 1 percent bonus for cashing any winning ticket, no matter where it was sold. . . .

Gambling-lotteries ads appear in every possible mass-marketing venue, television, radio, newspapers, Internet, billboards, buses. Giant jackpots, happy winners, and changed lives are news events. State-run lotteries are not subject to federal "truth in advertising" laws and are not subject, along with Indians, to Federal Communications Commission (FCC) bans against advertising. Advertising what was formerly sinful (betting) and illegal when conducted by individuals and is now lawful and "moral" when conducted by the state places the state in a strange and contradictory position. The state finds itself promoting a behavior, gambling, that is potentially dangerous for its citizens, or some of its citizens.

THE FEDERAL GOVERNMENT'S ROLE IN REGULATING GAMBLING

Denise von Herrmann

The regulation of gambling falls primarily under the jurisdiction of state governments. However, as Denise von Herrmann explains in the following article, the federal government has some regulatory power over interstate gambling matters and over Indian gaming. In addition, the federal courts have been called upon to rule in gambling cases that have either stymied state courts or exceeded their authority. Denise von Herrmann is a professor of political science at the University of Southern Mississippi. She has researched the gaming industry and authored *The Big Gamble: The Politics of Lottery and Casino Expansion*, from which this selection is taken.

The federal government of the United States has never played a major role in the regulation of gambling activity; the vast majority of legal gambling activity in the United States falls under state, and sometimes local, jurisdiction. Clearly, gambling is among the various morality policies placed within the state's jurisdiction by the police powers under the 10th Amendment to the U.S. Constitution.

While some say the federal government could, or should, take a greater role in gambling regulation, there are significant questions as to the constitutionality of any federal attempt to impose major new restrictions on gambling. Much depends on the technical legal framework in which one views gambling: Is it morality or is it commerce? Of course, gambling encompasses both concerns. It is quite clear that Congress has the firmly established authority to regulate most commerce. As early as 1824, the Supreme Court in *Gibbons v. Ogden* (22 U.S. 1) declared an expansive view of the Interstate Commerce Clause of the U.S. Constitution: "This power, like all others vested in Congress, is complete in itself, may be exercised to its utmost extent, and acknowledges no limitations, other than are prescribed in the constitution."

It is also clear that the states are considered primary in the regulation of activity deemed to be of a "moral" nature. Notable exceptions

Denise von Herrmann, *The Big Gamble: The Politics of Lottery and Casino Expansion*. Westport, CT: Praeger, 2002. Copyright © 2002 by Denise von Herrmann. All rights reserved. Reproduced by permission of Greenwood Publishing Group, Inc., Westport, CT.

to this general rule include the infamous federal attempt at alcohol prohibition and the current federal prohibitions on the use of illegal drugs. Far more examples of state authority over morality policies abound: from marriage and divorce laws to pornography and obscenity regulations to the rare cases such as Nevada where various forms of prostitution have been made legal. Overall, a far greater number of these examples show states taking the lead in morality regulations.

Even so, the federal government's general regulatory authority in the areas of taxation, interstate commerce, criminality, communications, and Indian affairs has created numerous opportunities for congressional, agency, and federal court actions in the area of gambling regulation. For example, when the National Gambling Impact Study Commission released its final report, it included a document listing all current federal regulations applicable to gambling or gaming. That document contains over 800 pages of federal statutes (National Gambling Impact Study Commission [NGISC], 1999). The commission was created by Congress in 1996 and was the third such national panel to be created by Congress in the past 60 years.

A search of Supreme Court cases involving some form of gambling, or relating to a gambling enterprise, has turned up 15 cases, dating back as far as the early 1800s. In 1850, for example, in *Phalen v. Virginia* (49 U.S.163), the Court expressed contempt for lotteries, calling them a form of "widespread pestilence." The *Champion v. Ames* (188 U.S.321) case, often referred to simply as "the lottery case," established in 1903 the Court's intention not to fully cede such cases to state courts, nor to relegate them exclusively to the area of "morality." The federal government continues to play an important, albeit secondary, role in gambling regulation. . . .

Regulating Gambling Devices and Activities

Much of the federal government's role in the regulation of gambling in the United States has occurred in the area of regulating the devices and paraphernalia associated with it. One of the first major pieces of such legislation was passed by Congress in the late 1940s. Section 1301 of the Federal Code prohibits the importation or transportation of illegal lottery tickets, either on one's person or via third-party carriers such as express delivery services.

Congress passed similar antigambling laws regarding casino devices beginning in 1951. The Gaming Devices Transportation Act was one in a series of laws passed during a period of intense scrutiny over illegal gambling that was carried out in various locations. These laws make it a federal crime to transport gambling devices such as slot machines into states where such machines are not legal and authorized by the state. . . .

Much of the impetus for these laws came from public hearings conducted by Senator Estes Kefauver (D-TN) during the 1950s. . . .

The Kefauver commission concentrated on illegal gambling activities in Illinois and Louisiana and on ties between legal and illegal gambling in Nevada as well. Concerns over the impact of organized crime were addressed, in part, in the nation's racketeering laws. Illegal gambling businesses are specifically included among the "unlawful activities" listed as part of the racketeering statutes. For purposes of the racketeering laws, gambling is described as "any business enterprise involving gambling . . . in violation of the laws of the State in which they are committed or of the United States" (96 USC Sect. 1961). The Organized Crime Control Act of 1970 also includes several prohibitions on illegal bookmaking and organized numbers games that often have been run by the mob (15 USC Sect. 1177).

The Federal Code includes prohibitions on the use of the postal system to facilitate gambling. Mailing lottery tickets, bookmaking information, and similar materials is a federal crime punishable by fines and possible jail time (18 USC Sect. 1301 and 1302). . . .

Recent attempts to curtail gambling under federal law include proposed bans on Internet gambling, and a law to make betting on all college sporting events illegal. The 1992 Professional and Amateur Sports Protection Act (28 USC Sect. 3702) forbids wagering on competitive sporting events such as college or professional sports, and forbids state and local governments from authorizing such activities, but it included a grandfather clause allowing states where such activities were then legal to continue offering sports betting. The proposed law (S. 2021 and H.R. 3575 of 1999–2000) would repeal the exceptions. Not surprisingly, legal sports book operators in Nevada have amassed tremendous resources in opposition to these bills.[1]

Regulations Pertaining to Gambling Locales

Congress, through its Interstate Commerce Clause powers, has also forbidden gambling in certain places and situations outright. For example, transportation regulations covering airlines prohibit the use of any form of gambling device on board aircraft used in international flights (49 USC Sect. 41311). Additional regulations stipulate the circumstances under which gambling may take place on board cruise ships and other vessels bound for international waters (26 USC Sect. 527). Generally, ships must be underway, not docked. . . .

Title 25 of the U.S. Code pertains to federal relations with Indian tribes and contains those sections of federal law allowing casinos on Indian lands. The 1988 Indian Gaming Regulatory Act [IGRA] (25 USC Sect. 2701) enables tribes to operate gaming on reservation property if the form of gambling is already legal in the state in which the reservation is located. The forms of gambling are divided into classes; it is Class III gambling (casinos, slot machines, and pari-mutuels of various

1. As of this writing, no action has been taken on either S.2021 or H.R. 3575.

kinds) that has become particularly prevalent.

Under the law, tribes may seek a compact to operate Class III gaming *of any kind* if *any other kind* of Class III gaming is legal within that state. Thus, for example, states with legal horse- or dog-racing tracks may become subject to the provisions when a tribe wishes to open a casino. . . .

Tribes must negotiate a compact with state officials, and several states have asserted that Congress overstepped the bounds of the 10th Amendment when it created a requirement that state governments enter into these negotiations with tribes. Thus far, however, the Supreme Court has upheld the 1988 law. . . .

Regulations Pertaining to Gambling Advertising

The Federal Communications Commission (FCC) has been given authority to regulate advertising on the nation's television and radio stations, yet Congress has chosen to make advertising gambling a part of the criminal code. Within the pertinent sections of the criminal code are several subsections pertaining specifically to advertisements for gambling establishments. The passages originally applied both to casino operations and to lotteries.

As state governments began to enact lotteries in an effort to generate revenues, the state lottery agencies began to seek an exemption from the criminal prohibition. Congress' response was to provide the exemption, but only for broadcasters in the same state where the lottery was located (18 USC Sect. 1304). The IGRA provides specific exemptions from Section 1304 for Indian casinos. A specific piece of legislation passed in 1988, the Charity Games Advertising Clarification Act (18 USC Sect. 1307), also exempts certain state-run and charitable casino games from the advertising bans—and extends those exemptions even to advertisements carried by stations in states where such activity is not legal.

The impact of these advertising bans, and the subsequent numerous and varied exemptions to them, has been to give the FCC (which effectively handles all cases of violations for the Solicitor General) broad power to decide what is, and is not, a legal advertisement for gambling. . . .

The Federal Courts' Role

The Supreme Court in 1999 made a dramatic change in federal public policies relating to gambling when it announced its ruling in *Greater New Orleans Broadcasting Association v. United States* (*GNOBA vs. U.S.* ([387 U.S. 98, 1999]). The 1999 decision decries the patchwork nature of federal regulations pertaining to gambling advertisements. It scolds Congress for the incoherence of its policies and declares that the existing regulations, as applied, arbitrarily condone some ads while prohibiting others of a very similar nature. "The federal government's regulations," said the Court, "neither reasonably promote important social goals nor accommodate competing State and private interests. All told," the Court added, "the FCC's policies regarding gambling advertising violate First Amendment protections of commercial speech" (*GNOBA v. U.S.*).

This was by no means the first time the U.S. Supreme Court had been asked to resolve disputes about gambling. Early case law, most of it from the 1950s, followed a flurry of federal activity aimed at eradicating illegal gambling, spurred by the actions of Senator Estes Kefauver and others. In *United States v. Korpan* (354 U.S. 271, 1957), the Supreme Court held that any coin-operated device that paid cash prizes was subject to the provisions of 26 USC, Sect. 4461, and a $25 per unit tax on gambling machines. The Court said the federal government had gone too far, however, when it required every manufacturer or dealer of gambling devices to meet certain reporting requirements or risk forfeiture of those devices even in cases in which interstate commerce was not appreciably affected (*United States v. Five Gambling Devices Etc.* [346 U.S. 441, 1953]).

The Court heard few gambling-related cases during the 1970s and 1980s. When the issue again arose, it did so in the form of Indian gaming. In 1987, the Court ruled that California had no legal authority to prohibit Indian tribes there to open and operate bingo halls or casinos, since other similar forms of gambling are allowable under California law (*California v. Cabazon Band of Mission Indians* [480 U.S. 202, 1987]).

Congress followed the decision by passing the Indian Gaming Regulatory Act in 1988 but controversies continued. The new law not only required states allowing gambling to enter into compacts with Indian tribes, but it also provided an avenue for tribes to sue, in federal court, states that refused to do so. The Seminole tribe in Florida did just that when, in 1991, the state refused to enter into compact negotiations. The Supreme Court said that Congress overstepped its boundaries in authorizing the lawsuits, since states are constitutionally protected from lawsuits by sovereign immunity (*Seminole Tribe of Florida v. Florida* [116 S.Ct. 1144, 1996]).

CHAPTER 2

INDIAN GAMING

Contemporary Issues
Companion

INDIAN GAMING BENEFITS NATIVE AMERICANS

Native American Report

In the following article, taken from *Native American Report*, the editors assert that Indian gaming has been an economic boon for participating tribes. While not all Native American tribes operate gambling enterprises, the authors report, those that run high-stakes bingo halls, card rooms, and casinos benefit from increased revenues and reduced employment. Tribal leaders contend that the financial rewards have led to improved utilities, greater educational opportunities, and the expansion of other social services. *Native American Report* is a newsletter that covers the latest issues in Indian affairs and serves as a forum for intertribal communication.

The concept of promoting gaming by a population known for more than its share of addiction problems may seem counterintuitive, but to hear tribal leaders tell the story, Indian gaming has been nothing short of a success story for the tribes that have embraced the idea.

"Why Indian gaming?" asked Ernie Stephens, chairman of the National Indian Gaming Association (NIGA). With its ability to generate high revenue and create jobs, "Indian gaming has done much to strengthen Indian and non-Indian communities around us," Stephens told a Sept. 20 [2004] Washington, D.C., briefing called to tell the Indian gaming story while thousands of Natives gathered in the nation's capital to celebrate the opening of the National Museum of the American Indian.

Indian gaming is now a $16.7 billion industry that has spawned 500,000 jobs, Stephens said. And it is not just Indians who have prospered: three-quarters of the employees are non-Indian.

"Our success extends beyond Indian reservations," Stephens said. Indian casinos pay above minimum wage and in some cases offer health benefits. Federal taxes amounting to $4.7 billion were paid in 2003, and jobs created by Indian gaming cut federal unemployment and welfare benefits by $1.2 billion, he said. In Indian Country, he said, "welfare-to-

Native American Report, "Indian Gaming: Tribal Leaders Tell of Benefits from Revenues," vol. 9, September 2004, p. 147. Copyright © 2004 by Business Publishers, Inc., www.bpinews.com. Reproduced by permission.

work worked." In addition, casinos have generated $100 million for local governments, he said, adding: "We pay our fair share."

Stephens and other speakers gamely refuted charges put forth in a recent *Wall Street Journal* article that lack of regulation is hindering clean operations at Indian casinos. Indian gaming faces three tiers of regulation—tribal, state and federal—that make it much more heavily regulated than either commercial gaming in Las Vegas and Atlantic City or state gaming such as lotteries and slot machines, according to Stephens and others.

The Possibilities

The stories told by the seven tribal leaders assembled at the briefing were tales of education, housing, social services and community development made possible by the dollars generated by casino tables and slot machines.

Doreen Hagen, president of the Prairie Island Indian Community in Minnesota, illustrated what Indian gaming has done for her small tribe. Coming from a childhood of abject poverty, she appeared visibly moved by the positive economic impact tribal gaming has had on her people. Close to three-quarters of adults are employed directly or indirectly by gaming, and others have begun businesses with gaming revenue.

The tribe now provides its own social services, operating out of a newly built community center, and provides health care to its people. In 1996, the tribe built a state-of-the-art water treatment facility—a situation "in stark contrast to my childhood when we didn't have running water," said Hagen. Last year the tribe established its own police department.

"Tribal gaming has given my people a political voice," she said. "Tribal gaming has allowed us once again to be contributors," she said. Prairie Island pays $10 million a year in state and federal taxes and since 1994 has contributed $12 million to local nonprofit and community groups, according to Hagen.

"Tribal gaming has allowed our tribe to regain our culture, tradition and language," she said. Religious and spiritual traditions are being practiced again and passed down to the children. To her, the bottom line is simple: "Indian gaming is truly an American success story."

Education and More

More success stories came from leaders of two larger tribes with major casino operations in Connecticut. Ironically, it is in the very "concentration of population that caused our history to be so, so heartbreaking that is now our patron base," said Michael Thomas, chairman of the Mashantucket Pequot Tribal Nation in Connecticut.

Gaming has funded essential community services that past Indian generations never would have dreamed of, Thomas said.

The tribe already provides cradle-to-grave education, and next it plans to build a school system so the tribe no longer will have to rely on Bureau of Indian Affairs schools—and so children will learn the language and "true history" of their people, he said. A child development center, with a newly added cultural center, already has been funded.

"We understand that knowledge, not slot machine revenue, is what's going to produce gains for the next generation," Thomas said.

The tribe provides health benefits for 40,000 lives, and between the Mashantucket and the nearby Mohegan Tribe, the two tribes pay state taxes that exceed the total combined corporate income tax paid in Connecticut, he said.

Job Opportunities

Were it not for these two tribes, Connecticut—which depended heavily on a defense industry that faltered—would have a 25 percent unemployment rate, according to Mohegan Chairman Mark Brown. Instead, the state has 4.5 percent unemployment, he said.

"What we have is a lot of tribes creating a lot of employment for people who didn't have it," said Jim Gray, chief of the Osage Tribe in Oklahoma.

In 1994, the Mohegan Tribe had $27 in the bank. "That was our tribal wealth." How times have changed. Now every tribal member can go to college, and elders—who should not want for anything—don't, he said.

"This is what Indian gaming can do not only for Indian people and other people, but for the government as well," said Thomas.

Gaming also has given rise to a political voice. For example, the Pechanga Band of Luiseno Indians in California was able to head off a power line plan that would have threatened the ecology of their lands, said Chairman Mark Macarro. "With Indian gaming, we're talking about being able to put some action behind the words of tribal sovereignty."

As in other tribes, gaming also has given the Pechangas the wherewithal to create an educational system that is once again bringing the Native language to the Native people, Macarro said.

Another View

Amid all the rosy pictures painted, Rosebud Sioux President Charlie Colombe gave what he called "the other side of the coin." Gaming on his reservation has been successful, he said, but not for economic reasons. With 25,000 members and $4 million in net annual profits from gaming, that works out to $160 per person, all of which goes into social service programs, he said.

But his vast South Dakota reservation, at 150 miles wide by 60 miles deep, still has only 20 police officers, a high crime rate, inadequate health care and 20,000 members living in poverty in the second-poorest county in the country.

The casino employs 160 people, which he said is a "huge success when you have 75 percent unemployment" and opens doors to starter jobs for young people. With the money generated, the tribe gives every child $100 with which to start school.

"As we go forward we need to look not only at the success of Indian gaming, but at the small things it does," said Colombe. In addition, he said, "I look to those tribes that have been very successful . . . they're stepping up and they're assisting tribes like ours."

Indeed, the Pechanga's Macarro said, now it is time to take things a step further to help each other more. Tribes need to work on building a national tribal economy by buying goods and services from each other, he suggested.

"We need to focus in Indian Country on goods and services provided by other tribes," Macarro said. "If we continue to do this, we can recycle dollars at least one more time in Indian Country." The goal, he said, should be to make 10 percent of all purchases from Indian Country.

In the end, the tribal leaders gathered were more than happy with what Indian gaming has done for their people—and happy about the museum festivities that brought Indian nations together for a week [in September 2004]. As Stephens said, "There's a lot of work to do . . . but this week we will celebrate."

INDIAN GAMING DOES NOT BENEFIT THE MAJORITY OF NATIVE AMERICANS

Donald L. Barlett and James B. Steele

In the following selection authors Donald L. Barlett and James B. Steele explain that the 1988 Indian Gaming Regulatory Act (IGRA), which gives qualifying Native American tribes the license to run gambling enterprises on reservation land, has unjustly enriched a few tribes that do not have to pay taxes on the billions of dollars reaped in revenues. As Barlett and Steele claim, this burgeoning industry is monopolized by a small percentage of America's tribes, leaving the vast majority of Native Americans in relative poverty. In addition, the authors argue, the money has given the newly rich tribes the power to influence federal politicians and thus keep the IGRA and other gaming policies from being revised or overturned. Barlett and Steele are Pulitzer Prize–winning investigative journalists working for *Time* magazine.

Imagine, if you will, Congress passing a bill to make Indian tribes more self-sufficient that gives billions of dollars to the white backers of Indian businesses—and nothing to hundreds of thousands of Native Americans living in poverty. Or a bill that gives hundreds of millions of dollars to one Indian tribe with a few dozen members—and not a penny to a tribe with hundreds of thousands of members. Or a bill that allows select Indian tribes to create businesses that reap millions of dollars in profits and pay no federal income tax—at the same time that the tribes collect millions in aid from American taxpayers. Can't imagine Congress passing such a bill? It did. Here's how it happened—and what it means.

Maryann Martin presides over America's smallest tribe. Raised in Los Angeles in an African-American family, she knew little of her Indian ancestry until 1986, when at age 22 she learned that her mother had been the last surviving member of the Augustine Band of Cahuilla Mission Indians. In 1991, the Bureau of Indian Affairs (BIA) certified Martin and her two younger brothers as members of the tribe. Federal recognition of tribal status opened the door for Martin and her siblings to qualify for certain types of government aid. And with it, a far more lucrative lure beckoned: the right to operate casinos on an Indian reservation.

As Indian casinos popped up like new housing developments across Southern California, Martin moved a trailer onto the long-abandoned Augustine reservation in Coachella, a 500-acre desert tract then littered with garbage, discarded household appliances and junk cars, about 25 miles southeast of Palm Springs. There she lived with her three children and African-American husband William Ray Vance. In 1994, membership in the tiny tribe dwindled from three adults to one when Martin's two brothers were killed during separate street shootings in Banning, Calif. Police said both men were involved in drug deals and were members of a violent Los Angeles street gang.

Subsequently, Martin negotiated a deal with Paragon Gaming, a Las Vegas company, to develop and manage a casino. Paragon is headed by Diana Bennett, a gaming executive and daughter of Vegas veteran and co-founder of the Circus Circus Casino William Bennett. Martin's Augustine Casino opened last July [2002]. With 349 slot machines and 10 gaming tables, it's the fifth and by far the most modest casino in the Palm Springs area. But it stands to make a lot of non-Indian investors—and one Indian adult—rich.

And get this: Martin still qualifies for federal aid, in amounts far greater than what many needy Native Americans could even dream of getting. In 1999 and 2000 alone, government audit reports show, she pulled in more than $1 million from Washington—$476,000 for housing, $400,000 for tribal government and $146,000 for environmental programs.

It wasn't supposed to be this way. At the end of the 1980s, in a frenzy of cost cutting and privatization, Washington perceived gaming on reservations as a cheap way to wean tribes from government handouts, encourage economic development and promote tribal self-sufficiency. After policy initiatives by the [Ronald] Reagan Administration and two U.S. Supreme Court rulings that approved gambling on Indian reservations, Congress enacted the Indian Gaming Regulatory Act in 1988. It was so riddled with loopholes, so poorly written, so discriminatory and subject to such conflicting interpretations that 14 years later, armies of high-priced lawyers are still debating the definition of a slot machine.

Instead of regulating Indian gambling, the act has created chaos and a system tailor-made for abuse. It set up a powerless and under-funded watchdog and dispersed oversight responsibilities among a hopelessly conflicting hierarchy of local, state and federal agencies. It created a system so skewed—only a few small tribes and their backers are getting rich—that it has changed the face of Indian country. Some long-dispersed tribes, aided by new, non-Indian financial godfathers, are regrouping to benefit from the gaming windfall. Others are seeking new reservations—some in areas where they never lived, occasionally even in other states—solely to build a casino. And leaders of small, newly wealthy tribes now have so much unregulated cash and political clout that they can ride roughshod over neighboring communities, poorer tribes and even their own members.

The amount of money involved is staggering. Last year 290 Indian casinos in 28 states pulled in at least $12.7 billion in revenue. Of that sum, *Time* estimates, the casinos kept more than $5 billion as profit. That would place overall Indian gaming among *Fortune* magazine's 20 most profitable U.S. corporations, with earnings exceeding those of [large financial institutions such as] J.P. Morgan Chase & Co., Merrill Lynch, American Express and Lehman Bros. Holdings combined.

But who, exactly, is benefiting? Certainly Indians in a few tribes have prospered. In California, Christmas came early this year for the 100 members of the Table Mountain Rancheria, who over Thanksgiving picked up bonus checks of $200,000 each as their share of the Table Mountain Casino's profits. That was in addition to the monthly stipend of $15,000 each member receives. But even those amounts pale beside the fortunes made by the behind-the-scenes investors who bankroll the gaming palaces. They walk away with up to hundreds of millions of dollars.

Meanwhile, the overwhelming majority of Indians get nothing. Only half of all tribes—which have a total of 1.8 million members— have casinos. Some large tribes like the Navajo oppose gambling for religious reasons. Dozens of casinos do little better than break even because they are too small or located too far from population centers. The upshot is that a small number of gaming operations are making most of the money. [In 2001] just 39 casinos generated $8.4 billion. In short, 13% of the casinos accounted for 66% of the take. All of which helps explain why Indian gaming has failed to raise most Native Americans out of poverty. What has happened instead is this:

A Losing Hand

Revenue from gaming is so lopsided that Indian casinos in five states with almost half the Native American population—Montana, Nevada, North Dakota, Oklahoma and South Dakota—account for less than 3% of all casino proceeds. On average, they produce the equivalent of about $400 in revenue per Indian. Meanwhile, casinos in California, Connecticut and Florida—states with only 3% of the Indian population—haul in 44% of all revenue, an average of $100,000 per Indian. In California, the casino run by the San Manuel Band of Mission Indians pulls in well over $100 million a year. That's about $900,000 per member.

The Rich Get Richer

While federal recognition entitles tribes to a broad range of government benefits, there is no means testing. In 2001, aid to Indians amounted to $9.4 billion, but in many cases more money went to wealthy members of tribes with lucrative casinos than to destitute Indians. From 1995 to 2001, the Indian Health Service, the agency responsible for looking after the medical needs of Native Americans, spent an average of $2,100 a year on each of the 2,800 members of the Seminole tribe in Florida. The Seminoles' multiple casinos generated $216 million in profits [in 2001], and each tribe member collected $35,000 in casino dividends. During the same six years, the health service spent an annual average of just $470 on each of the 52,000 members of the Muscogee (Creek) Nation in Oklahoma, whose tiny casinos do little more than break even.

Buying Politicians

Wealthy Indian gaming tribes suddenly are pouring millions of dollars into political campaigns at both state and federal levels. They are also influencing gaming and other policies affecting Native Americans by handing out large sums to influential lobbying firms. In 2000 alone, tribes spent $9.5 million on Washington lobbying. Altogether they spend more to influence legislation than such longtime heavyweights as General Motors, Boeing, AT&T—or even Enron in its heyday.

Gaming Tribes as Exclusive Clubs

Tribal leaders are free to set their own whimsical rules for admission, without regard to Indian heritage. They may exclude rivals, potential whistle-blowers and other legitimate claimants. The fewer tribe members, the larger the cut for the rest. Some tribes are booting out members, while others are limiting membership. Among them: the Pechanga Band of Mission Indians in Riverside County, Calif., whose new Las Vegas–style gaming palace, the Pechanga Resort & Casino, is expected to produce well over $100 million in revenue.

Gold Rush

Since only a federally recognized tribe can open a casino, scores of groups—including long-defunct tribes and extended families—have flocked to the BIA or Congress seeking certification. Since 1979, as gambling has boomed, the number of recognized tribes on the U.S. mainland has spiked 23%, to a total of 337. About 200 additional groups have petitioned the bureau for recognition. Perhaps the most notorious example of tribal resurrection: the Mashantucket Pequots of Connecticut, proud owners of the world's largest casino, Foxwoods. The now billion-dollar tribe had ceased to exist until Congress recreated it in 1983. The current tribe members had never lived together on a reservation. Many of them would not even qualify for government assistance as Indians.

Congress created the National Indian Gaming Commission (NIGC) to be the Federal Government's principal oversight-and-enforcement agency for Indian gaming—and then guaranteed that it could do neither. With a budget capped at $8 million, the agency has 63 employees to monitor the $12.7 billion all-cash business in more than 300 casinos and small gaming establishments nationwide. The New Jersey Casino Control Commission, by contrast, has a $59 million budget and a staff of 720 to monitor 12 casinos in Atlantic City that produce one-third the revenue. The NIGC has yet to discover a single major case of corruption—despite numerous complaints from tribe members.

The White Man Wins Again

While most Indians continue to live in poverty, many non-Indian investors are extracting hundreds of millions of dollars—sometimes in violation of legal limits—from casinos they helped establish, either by taking advantage of regulatory loopholes or cutting backroom deals. More than 90% of the contracts between tribes and outside gaming-management companies operate with no oversight. That means investors' identities are often secret, as are their financial arrangements and their share of the revenue. Whatever else Congress had in mind when it passed the regulatory act, presumably the idea was not to line the pockets of a Malaysian gambling magnate, a South African millionaire or a Minnesota leather-apparel king.

Fraud, Corruption, Intimidation

The tribes' secrecy about financial affairs—and the complicity of government oversight agencies—has guaranteed that abuses in Indian country growing out of the surge in gaming riches go undetected, unreported and unprosecuted. Tribal leaders sometimes rule with an iron fist. Dissent is crushed. Cronyism flourishes. Those who question how much the casinos really make, where the money goes or even tribal operations in general may be banished. Indians who challenge the system are often intimidated, harassed and threatened with reprisals or physical harm. They risk the loss of their jobs, homes and income. Margarite Faras, a member of the San Carlos Apache tribe, which owns the Apache Gold Casino in San Carlos, Ariz., was ousted from the tribal council after exposing corruption that led to the imprisonment of a former tribal leader. For three years, Faras says, those in control mounted nighttime demonstrations at her home, complete with loudspeakers. They initiated a boycott of her taco business, telling everyone she used cat meat. They telephoned her with death threats. Says Faras: "I don't know what else to say, other than it's been a nightmare."

THE MEDIA PROMOTE AN UNJUST BACKLASH AGAINST INDIAN GAMING

Katherine A. Spilde

In December 2002 *Time* magazine published a series of articles claiming that Indian gaming does not benefit most Native Americans but instead profits a few wealthy tribes that have powerful political influence. In the following rebuttal to this series and other articles critical of Indian gaming, Katherine A. Spilde argues that the media have created a false image of "rich Indians" who circumvent laws to make themselves wealthy at the expense of their nongaming brethren. In fact, Spilde maintains, the federal government has endorsed the right of gaming tribes to operate gambling facilities, and many of these tribes share their revenues with nongaming tribes. Spilde also claims that the proceeds from tribal gaming are making tangible improvements in Native American culture, including political power that Indians have long been denied. In Spilde's view, the media-created backlash against Indian gaming is meant to undermine tribal sovereignty and foster a popular belief that gaming tribes are undeserving of their legally acquired wealth. Katherine A. Spilde, a senior research associate at Harvard University's Kennedy School of Government, studies tribal economic issues. She has served as a board member on the National Council on Problem Gambling.

On December 16, 2002, *Time Magazine* ran a cover story on Indian gaming called "Wheel of Misfortune: Why Indian Casinos Aren't All They're Promised to Be." This story, the first in a two-part series, claimed to be an "investigative report" into the Indian Gaming Regulatory Act (IGRA) and the impacts of Indian gaming. The second part of the *Time* series, "Playing the Political Slots: How Indian Casino Interests Have Learned the Art of Buying Influence in Washington," appeared a week later. The authors, senior editors at *Time*, heavily promoted the series on television and radio for the weeks after its publication. While new in its national reach, the *Time* series is simply one more diatribe in the cycle of misinformation about Indian gaming. This time, however, tribal sovereignty itself is the target.

At first blush, the main thrust of the first *Time Magazine* article seems to be that Indian gaming is loosely regulated by the National Indian Gaming Commission, allowing non-Indian investors to skirt federal laws in order to become the primary beneficiaries of Indian gaming. This is not a new claim, and it is easy to refute with the facts. The second *Time* article trotted out the ever-popular story that some tribal governments are making political contributions and that they are trying to influence policy-making, a story that has little to add to the debate about Indian gaming's impacts and documents perfectly legal behavior.

The Danger of Playing on Popular Sentiment

What is dangerous about the *Time* series and distinguishes it from its predecessors, however, is that it develops and naturalizes a very popular and precarious claim that plays on America's emotions. Throughout the series, the authors use selective reporting and speculation to build an argument that there are now two separate classes of American Indian people: those who are becoming wealthy from Indian gaming and those who are not. Here we get to the heart of the matter: *Time* has found a new (perhaps slightly more creative) way to create a category in American's minds—the so-called "Rich Indian"—in order to call into question the rights of all tribal governments to exercise their sovereign right to engage in gaming. What is interesting about the *Time* article is not that it makes this argument, but how it does so—and why.

The "Rich Indian" Stereotype

While the idea that there are now "rich Indians" is not new, the *Time* articles have employed this stereotype in a way that is intended to undermine tribal sovereignty in general and Indian gaming in particular. The *Time* series, like others before it, relies upon generalizations to strengthen the inaccurate but popular notion that somehow Indian gaming is not benefiting a sufficient number of American Indians—or the right (i.e. deserving) ones. It recycles a number of familiar but constant themes that take on a certain legitimacy in the public's mind simply because they continue to be raised. Throughout the series, the authors emphasize the disparity between "poor" and "needy" tribes and "wealthy Indian gaming tribes" who are sometimes also characterized as "long defunct" or "re-created." These extreme depictions serve a dual purpose: to first create and then naturalize the categories of "real Indians," who continue to suffer, and so-called "rich Indians," who are depicted as not suffering and, at times, of questionable Indian identity. It is the latter group that *Time* characterizes as "the few who have casino riches" due to their "money-churning casinos."

Documenting the fact that some tribal governments are benefiting more than others from Indian gaming is not a newsworthy finding since it simply reflects the fact that Indian gaming facilities have differential access to markets and, consequently, uneven revenues. Rather, these authors develop a not-so-subtle argument that these discrepancies are wrong. While these portrayals are clearly meant to engage the emotions of *Time*'s readers, they also serve a pointed political function: to depict Indian gaming as a federal Indian "policy problem" in dire need of a "policy solution." The articles read like a laundry list of accusations about Indian gaming regulation, tribal government jurisdiction, American Indian identity, the federal recognition process, management relationships, campaign contributions and taxation policy. By reducing Indian gaming to two competing stereotypes—the "rich Indian" and the long-suffering "real Indian"—the *Time* articles have the potential (and may be intentioned) to undermine Indian gaming's political foundation by diminishing the public support for Indian gaming while simultaneously justifying the favored political "solution" of anti-Indian policy makers.

The Influence of the Media

Journalists know and scholars reveal that there is a clear relationship between what is called "media agenda setting" and "policy agenda setting." While media does not tell the American public what to think, it does tell them what to think about. In that way, media drives public opinion, which in turn influences what policy makers care about and how they speak publicly on certain issues. Given this dynamic, there is a direct relationship between media portrayals of American Indian people and both public opinion and federal Indian policy.

One need not look beyond William Safire's December 12, 2002, *New York Times* piece, "Tribes of Gamblers," to appreciate the political usefulness (and potential danger) of the ideas recycled in the *Time* series. Safire repeats much of *Time*'s original material but takes the argument a step further by calling upon particular policy makers not only to triple the funding for the National Indian Gaming Commission (at tribal expense, of course) but also to hold hearings on what he calls "a scandal rooted in the manipulation of Congress." Importantly, Safire's article can be read as direct support for Rep. Frank Wolf of Virginia, a gambling opponent who has repeatedly argued that Congress form a "Study Commission" to investigate Indian gaming's impacts. (Incidentally, when Congressman Wolf first offered his legislation, he referenced a series of articles in the *Boston Globe* to support his claims that Indian gaming "is not working.")

But do the reporters at *Time* or *The New York Times* (or Frank Wolf, for that matter) really care about American Indian communities or individuals who continue to suffer? Are they using their political clout to call upon the federal government to fully fund federal programs, implement effective trust reform policies and fulfill treaty obligations? Are they encouraging policy solutions to poverty in Indian Country? No. Why? Because these articles are not about Indian poverty at all; they are about Indian power. More to the point, they are about the growth of the tribes' potential collective political influence and about finding ways to diminish it.

Targeting Tribal Sovereignty

The first installment of the *Time* article shows its hand in a section called "Buying Politicians." Here, the reader is told that, "Wealthy Indian gaming tribes suddenly are pouring millions of dollars into political campaigns at both state and federal levels. They are also influencing gaming and other policies affecting Native Americans by handing out large sums to influential lobbying firms." The second part takes the argument further by stating that not only is Indian gaming unevenly distributed, but those tribes that are benefiting from gaming exert a "disproportionate clout" in Washington, D.C.

Ultimately, *Time*'s concern is not with Indian gaming's uneven distribution or with "rich Indians." Rather, these articles are concerned with the ways that tribal governments are influencing legislation that until recently was created "on their behalf" rather than with their needs in mind or with their input. *Time* is saying that tribal rights and tribal sovereignty are tolerable as long as they are symbolic; that tribal governments deserve federal support and public sympathy as long as they continue to struggle. However, now that many tribal governments are beginning to set their own agendas, the cycle of misinformation begins again in order to convince the American public that tribes no longer need or deserve tribal sovereignty or Indian gaming.

For some Americans, the *Time* agenda is an easy sell. The fact that tribal governments are slowly changing the system that once excluded them has not been popular among some anti-Indian groups, whether political opponents or business competitors. Understanding the *Time* series as a response to increasing tribal empowerment reveals the paradox that tribes have already experienced: that as they exert more power in Congress or in their respective states, they become more vulnerable to vicious media attacks. As tribal governments continue to exercise their inherent sovereignty, it seems clear that their opponents feel compelled to intensify their attempts to undermine the overwhelming popular support for tribal governments. Just as the balance of power has changed, the political backlash against Indian gaming has shifted from one focused strictly on the bottom line to a battle over public perception and public sentiment. Both sides understand that the scope of tribal sovereignty itself may be at stake.

Scholars affiliated with the Harvard Project on American Indian Economic Development [HPAIED] have called tribal sovereignty, "the great development asset Indian nations possess." In their work on economic development in Indian country, HPAIED researchers consistently find that when tribal governments can effectively exercise their sovereignty, "they can turn it from a legal condition or rhetorical claim into a practical tool for nation building." This assertion that tribal sovereignty is the crucial underpinning for tribal political power is right on point; why else would *Time* and others work so hard to argue that tribal sovereignty itself is the problem, not the solution?

The Truth About Gaming's Benefits

What is most disappointing about the *Time* series and others like it is that these pieces miss the opportunity to tell an even better story: the truth. Tribal sovereignty, when acknowledged and supported by self-determination policies, can be mobilized to build strong and healthy Indian nations. Academic research reveals that Indian gaming in particular is having profound economic and social impacts across many parts of Indian Country, allowing tribal governments to begin to heal the deep suffering caused by centuries of harmful federal policies and funding shortfalls.

Time could have told the story of the Pechanga Tribe of Luiseno Indians in California, who have hired a full-time linguist to teach the Luiseno language in their new pre-school. Or the story of the Mohegan Tribe in Connecticut, who are diversifying their economic base by reviving the aquaculture program that sustained them in their traditional economy. Or, the San Manuel Band of Serrano Mission Indians in California, who donated $1 million to the White Mountain Apache Tribe in Arizona when the Apache's reservation was devastated by a wildfire [in fall 2001].

By focusing on issues that support a particular political agenda, *Time* has overlooked the most compelling story of them all: for the first time since Europeans arrived, tribal governments are strengthening their economies and fully exercising their inherent sovereign rights. But perhaps that is the point; because the renaissance of American Indian cultures actually benefits American Indian people, unfortunately, it is not yet considered newsworthy in its own right.

ABUSING TRIBAL SOVEREIGNTY TO PROMOTE INDIAN GAMING

Jan Golab

In the following article investigative journalist Jan Golab argues that the federal government's recognition of Indian tribal sovereignty has allowed Native American tribes to evade laws that apply to the rest of Americans. Golab examines the tribal gaming industry, for example, and points out how Native American tribes that run gaming enterprises are exempt from having their revenues taxed. Few non-Indians, Golab notes, see the justice in tolerating the loss of billions of dollars in untaxed Indian wealth. According to Golab, Native Americans also abuse tribal sovereignty when small, unofficial tribes sue for federal recognition so that they can open casinos without concern for gambling's impact on the broader community. Antigambling campaigns, which have sprung up in response to the rise of Indian gaming, have met with little success at keeping the casinos at bay, Golab maintains, since the gaming tribes can shield themselves behind their federally recognized right to manage their own affairs. Golab is a California author who has covered Indian gaming since 1983.

Foxwoods, the King Kong of casinos, was brought to Connecticut with dreams of untold riches. Now, locals are trying to kill the beast. Foxwoods and its sister institution, Mohegan Sun, (the world's two most profitable casinos), pay host state Connecticut a hefty $400 million a year—one fourth of the take. Yet in 2003, Connecticut became the first state in the country to pass legislation designed to halt any future casino development. The measure passed unanimously, not exactly a ringing endorsement for Indian gambling institutions. "Another gambling palace anywhere in the state would be disastrous," the *Hartford Courant* warned in an editorial. "The state must stop this slot-machine tsunami."

Jeff Benedict is president of the Connecticut Alliance Against

Casino Expansion, and the author of *Without Reservation*, a book about the Mashantucket Pequot Indians and their Foxwoods casino. "Casino money costs us a lot more than it's worth," Benedict argues. He recites a litany of woes: Casinos have a negative impact on roads, water and land consumption, fire, police, ambulance service, air pollution, and traffic. Local school systems are flooded with the children of low-income casino workers, who also create a shortage of affordable housing. And there are social costs—increased bankruptcies, foreclosures, divorces, child abuse, and crime. "The closer a community gets to a casino, the higher those numbers are," says Benedict. "Who pays for that? The local and state governments."

Casinos cause property devaluation and lost taxes when businesses and lands are taken over by tax-exempt tribes. While casino owners argue that they create jobs and help neighboring businesses, the casinos (which, as Indian enterprises, do not have to pay the same taxes or abide by the same laws as other establishments) actually damage competing businesses nearby—restaurants, bars, hotels, retail outlets. "When the Indian casino comes to town, nobody else does well," says Benedict.

Except for the lawyers. The Pequots have subjected their host state and local governments to a decade of legal battles over tribal land annexation, environmental and land-use regulations, and sovereign immunity from lawsuits and police jurisdiction. Local communities have spent millions litigating against further casino expansion. Twelve more would-be "tribes" are petitioning the Bureau of Indian Affairs for federal tribal status, and new land claims threaten over one third of Connecticut's real estate.

Resurrected Tribes and New Reservations

Another book on Foxwoods, *Hitting the Jackpot*, by *Wall Street [Journal]* reporter Brett Fromson, explains how a "tribe" that disappeared 300 years ago resurrected itself and won a gambling monopoly now worth $1.2 billion a year. Like Benedict, Fromson concludes that the recreated Pequot tribe is illegitimate, a political contrivance based on sympathy and political correctness, not reality or common sense— "the greatest legal scam."

Next door in New York, the situation is even worse. The Empire State approved the Oneida Nation's Turning Stone Casino near Oneida ten years ago, without first obtaining any agreement for the Nation to share its revenues ($232 million in 2001) with the state, or any agreement to settle the tribe's claim to 250,000 acres of central New York land. Subsequent casino compacts with other tribes have been haphazard and subject to ongoing renegotiation, with New York collecting money from some, not from others.

The Oneidas have used their casino cash machine to buy 16,000 acres of land and businesses, including nearly all of the area's gasoline and convenience stores. Once they are Indian-owned, the land and businesses go off the tax rolls. The business impact and loss of property and sales taxes has some local communities teetering on bankruptcy. "The tribes hurt us in a number of ways," explains Scott Peterman, president of Upstate Citizens for Equality. "They buy a property and refuse to pay property tax because they say they are re-acquiring their ancient reservation. Then they open a business on that property and refuse to collect sales tax."

By undercutting all non-Indian businesses that collect taxes, tribal sales of gasoline and cigarettes alone cost New York state millions of dollars in annual taxes. The Supreme Court ruled in 1994 that states could tax tribal sales to non-native customers, but so far, New York has failed to enforce this over Indian resistance. One tribe, the Onondaga, sells an estimated 20,000 cartons of cigarettes every week, or $26 million worth a year. Governor George Pataki tried to collect in 1997, but he backed down when Indian protestors blocked the New York State Thruway. . . .

The state with the most tribal casinos—82—is Oklahoma, where tribes rake in as much as $1.2 billion a year—and the state doesn't get a cent. Oklahoma Indians, who comprise 7 percent of the state population, have become the most powerful political force there. Meanwhile, officials estimate that Oklahoma's 39 tribes cost the state $500 million a year—in lost property taxes, lost revenues on tax-free cigarettes, and lost excise taxes and tag fees from cars sold by reservation dealerships. That's nearly the equivalent of the state's 2003 budgetary shortfall, enough to pay for 17,000 teachers. Meanwhile, the state's billion-dollar racetrack industry, which does pay taxes, is teetering on the edge of bankruptcy, and communities are mired in litigation with cash-flush tribes over land and water rights.

False Sovereignty

As Connecticut, New York, and Oklahoma wrestle to control their Indian casinos, California's casinos are rapidly expanding, and many other states, like Pennsylvania and Maryland, are just gearing up. Governor Arnold Schwarzenegger's legacy will largely be a matter of whether or not he allows the Golden State to become the new Nevada. With their state monopoly on gambling, California Indians could eventually become the richest people on earth. Their 54 casinos are already raking in $5 billion a year, which isn't far behind the entire Las Vegas area ($7.7 billion), and they are pushing for more. With 107 federally recognized Indian reservations and rancherias—more than anywhere else in the country—California could easily surpass Nevada as the nation's gambling capital in the next few years.

Yet tribal chairmen blast the California governor for suggesting that they "pay their fair share." They insist that: "Governments cannot tax other governments!" They insist they are "sovereign."

"Sovereign" usually means "independent." American Indians, however, are completely dependent on their host governments—for roads, power, water, fire and police protection, schools, universities, hospitals, and health care facilities. "The technical term for Indian reservations is 'domestic dependent nations,'" explains one legislative analyst. "They are not foreign governments. They have no foreign policy powers. They are not allowed to sell their land to anyone outside the U.S. and they are not allowed to maintain relations with any foreign nation. To regard them as being like foreign nations inside our nation is very problematic. How can Congress create a government within a state, with powers that Congress itself could never possess?"

The notion that American Indian tribes should be treated like Canada or France, as some tribal leaders assert, offends common sense. "A nation within the nation" is what they claim to be, but it is not even close to a reality. If they are independent nations, why have Indians been allowed to donate over $150 million to U.S. political campaigns and become our nation's most influential political special interest group?

Reservation Shopping

Californians have already shown their disgust for the "pay-to-play" politics that linked Indians to ousted governor Gray Davis and his lieutenant governor Cruz Bustamante, who did the Indians' bidding while taking $12 million of their cash. Experts say that is only the tip of the iceberg. Senator Barbara Boxer (D-California) and Representatives George Miller (D-Richmond), Mary Bono (R-Palm Springs), Hilda Solis (D-East L.A.), and Joe Baca (D-San Bernardino) have long served as legislative activists to expand tribal sovereignty. They have pushed through legislation to recognize "tribes" so they can avoid a lengthy and complicated federal recognition process that includes oversight by the governor and secretary of the interior. This form of "reservation shopping" via sympathetic legislation is responsible for many new gambling resorts.

Senator Boxer pushed a bill through Congress granting federal recognition to the Federated Coast Miwoks of Graton Rancheria, a small landless "tribe," after receiving assurances they would not open a casino. But then the tribe hired a team of advisers, including Boxer's son Doug, and announced plans for a massive $100 million Nevada-financed casino and resort in California's wine country. Four city council members in Rohnert Park, the proposed site of the resort, are now facing a grassroots recall for selling out to the Indians.

Another small tribe, the 70-member Ione Band of Miwok Indians, had no interest in pursuing a casino until the tribe was hijacked by officials from the U.S. Bureau of Indian Affairs [BIA]. These agents, in a move not uncommon in the murky world of Indian politics, opened the tribe's membership rolls against the wishes of the tribal leadership and added 450 new members, including the BIA officials themselves and their families. These new "tribal members" then called for an election and overthrew the existing tribal leadership. The BIA officials not only made themselves members of a tribe they were administering, they took it over—for the purpose of promoting (and profiting from) a $100 million casino in Plymouth, California. Four members of Congress have called for an investigation into the Ione Miwok takeover. . . .

"The debate over Indian sovereignty may seem abstract," explains one analyst, "but it gets very concrete when a state suddenly loses authority over a major portion of its land. Reservation shopping basically gives wealthy gambling tribes the ability to shrink counties and states"—and to place important personal actions and economic transactions beyond the reach of American law. Throughout the nation, whenever U.S. citizens battle tribes over problems with land, water, zoning disputes, personal injuries, firings, broken contracts, or other issues, the claim of tribal sovereignty often intervenes. As tribal governments expand, local governments lose their political power to protect their citizens, some of whom find themselves ruined by tribal sovereignty claims—like the rancher who lost all his water to a new tribal golf course and resort.

The Citizens Equal Rights Alliance and United Property Owners, umbrella organizations encompassing hundreds of grassroots groups affected by Indian sovereignty claims, represent some 3.5 million citizens and business and property owners affected by America's 550-plus Indian reservations. There are also independent organizations in 22 states, like One Nation in Oklahoma, Upstate Citizens for Equality in New York, and Stand Up for California.

Activists in this rapidly growing anti-sovereignty movement feel betrayed by their elected leaders. Indian sovereignty, they say, is a profoundly flawed special body of federal law—some say an outright scam—that creates bogus tribes, legalizes race-based monopolies, creates a special class of super-citizens immune to the laws that govern others, and Balkanizes America. "Sovereign rights based on race for a few American citizens is not, and will never be, reconcilable with the equality and civil rights guaranteed by the United States Constitution to all citizens," says Scott Peterman, of Upstate Citizens for Equality. "The concepts of equal rights, equal opportunities, equality under the law, and equal responsibilities for all citizens should not be bargained away by our politicians."

The Abuses of IGRA

Many say that sovereignty is a concept from another age that no longer works today. "It goes back a century to when native populations had been dispossessed," explains former California senator Pete Wilson, "to when the U.S. was largely an agricultural nation and we did not have the kind of economy we have today." Wilson says that when the Indian Gaming Regulatory Act (IGRA) was enacted in 1988, it didn't get nearly the attention it deserved. "A lot of people [in Congress] voted for it thinking that it amounted to little more than Bingo on reservations. . . . They didn't see it as a commercial enterprise that would transform reservations and their surrounding communities."

Most analysts concur that IGRA is a terrible law—vague, fuzzy, and unclear. "Congress should have spelled out much more clearly what the tribes are allowed to do," explains one analyst. "IGRA has subsequently been interpreted by the courts to mean that a state can pass a ballot initiative granting a lucrative monopoly on gambling, based solely on race, within a state that does not otherwise allow gambling. It defies the basic principles of equal protection, and gives cause to wonder. Should we give Hispanics the liquor industry? Should blacks get cigarettes? What about the Asian boat people?"

IGRA became a mechanism for the gambling industry to enter states where gambling had been illegal for more than a century, allowing it to operate outside the legal jurisdiction of the state governments. It pitted tribes against tribes, and tribal leaders against their own members, and created impossible entanglements of governance and jurisdiction. IGRA essentially created an attractive investment opportunity for the gaming industry, much as minority-contracting rules created an industry out of finding black and Hispanic figurehead partners with which to pursue government contracts. The potential gambling revenues made it attractive for marginal groups to seek tribal status, specifically for the purpose of opening a gaming franchise. "The groups in some cases are so marginal it's almost laughable," says one legislative analyst. "Often they are subdivisions of actual tribes—the left-fork wing of the old river Indian tribe. It's not about tribal identity. What they really want is a casino."

Experts contend that Congress never intended sovereign status for every parcel of land granted to Indians. The small California rancherias, for example, were meant to host housing projects for landless Indians. One such group of federal housing recipients-turned-Indian-tribe, the Auburns, have used their new sovereign status to open the massive Thunder Valley casino near Sacramento. The Auburns are descendants of 40 Indians who were set up on a few dozen acres of public housing in 1910. "Do you really think Congress intended for them to be a sovereign nation over which state law would have no force?" asks one legislative analyst who specializes in Indian law.

Congress's Problem

Scott Peterman says the Indian sovereignty problem will ultimately have to be solved by Congress, a sentiment echoed by many other observers across the nation. "They are the ones who created the mess," says Peterman. He believes Congress should terminate tribal sovereignty definitively. "The irony is, the tribes claim they need sovereignty to preserve their culture, but they use it to build casinos. They talk about 'mother earth,' but they are more than willing to trade land for slot machines. Many tribal governments are so corrupt they are a bigger enemy to Indian culture than anybody. The Amish, Quakers, and Mennonites preserve their culture better than any Indian tribe, and they do it while paying taxes. Indians don't need sovereignty, or a whole federal bureau, to maintain their culture."

For many years, the Supreme Court avoided the big questions and made up Indian law by carving off issues piecemeal. In 1998, the Court concluded that the doctrine of tribal sovereign immunity was outdated, but it also concluded that Congress, not the courts, needed to fix it.

President [George W.] Bush has at least moved to halt the march toward expanded sovereignty. Several tribes pushed President [Bill] Clinton to enact more-liberal rules that would have made it even easier for tribes to reservation shop. President Bush withdrew those relaxed rules. Tom Grey, director of the National Coalition Against Gambling Expansion, advised President Bush in a 2003 letter that "if pending approval of more than 200 self-described 'Indian Tribes' is not denied, there will be a veritable explosion of gambling emporiums throughout America, threatening local economies, increasing addiction and concomitant criminality, and disrupting social and political stability."

When it comes to sovereignty, everyone seems to agree that Congress will eventually have to "mend it or end it." Congress has the power to shape and re-shape the relevant laws as it sees fit. The problem is a lack of will, due largely to ignorance or fear of the fast-growing political clout of tiny gambling-enriched tribes who have shown a great willingness to use their lucre for political donations. . . .

Many experts believe it will take years before the inevitable day of reckoning on sovereignty finally reaches the halls of Congress. But the public mood is changing rapidly in certain places. Some observers believe this subject could mature into a bona fide political issue much sooner.

As executive director of United Property Owners and a national spokesperson for One Nation, Barb Lindsay represents more than 300,000 property owners, scores of grassroots community groups, dozens of local governments, and thousands of small businesses. Part Indian herself, Lindsay has been lobbying in Washington for ten years. She has emerged as one of the leading voices in the growing national movement challenging tribal sovereignty.

"Five years ago, people didn't know anything about tribal sovereignty," Lindsay explains. "Indian gaming has really elevated the issue in terms of public awareness, and with elected officials and their staffs. A few years ago they were not very sympathetic to our cause, because all they knew was tribal positions. But with growing problems in states like Connecticut, California, Wisconsin, New York, Oregon,

Washington, and Oklahoma, more Congressmen are having problems in their own districts. They see tribes running roughshod over local citizens, ignoring environment laws and land-use codes and water rights. Instead of the *Dances with Wolves* Hollywood mythology they've been sold, they are now facing the reality of dealing with a group of people who believe they are somehow above the law."

The true meaning of sovereignty, Lindsay says, is tax evasion. "It is no coincidence that the states now facing the biggest budget deficits are also the states with the largest number of tax-exempt Indian casinos and tax-evading tribal businesses. It is widely recognized that IGRA is being abused and Indian casino reservation shopping is undermining local, county, and state tax bases and changing community character and quality of life, while simultaneously denying local citizens a voice in how the future of their community will be shaped."

THE BACKLASH AGAINST INDIAN GAMING IN CALIFORNIA

Jim Doyle

Jim Doyle is a staff writer for the *San Francisco Chronicle*. In the following article Doyle reports on the growing backlash against Indian gaming in California. Many California voters once endorsed gaming as a means to help the state's tribes become more self-sufficient, Doyle writes. However, as the number of casinos raking in billions of tax-free dollars grows, California voters now worry that their state could become an undesirable gambling mecca. Especially troubling, Doyle notes, is the practice of "reservation shopping," whereby formerly landless tribes acquire property near cities and then build casinos on this new "reservation" land. Detractors contend that once gambling halls spring up close to population centers, a host of social ills—from crime to increased incidents of problem gambling—will soon follow, Doyle reports. Wary of these drawbacks, Californians are beginning to take a stand against the further spread of Indian gaming.

Twenty minutes west of Palm Springs [California], a glittering 23-story skyscraper towers over a tranquil canyon in the bone-dry desert. The Morongo Band of Mission Indians' new $250 million casino, resort and spa is almost completed, and the once poor, 1,000-member tribe plans to erect a second casino.

On the Rumsey Rancheria near Woodland (Yolo County) [California], the Rumsey Band of Wintun Indians have expanded their Cache Creek Casino Resort, adding a 200-room hotel that overlooks the Capay Valley. The tribe has built luxury homes for their 23 adult members, a school for the tribe's children, and a community center.

None of the Rumsey Band's members is on welfare, but some California tribes with casinos are not faring as well. The Chato Tribe of the Laytonville Rancheria ekes out a living in rural Mendocino County from less than 100 slot machines at its tiny Red Fox Casino. And near the gates of the Konocti Vista Casino in Lake County, members of the Big Valley Band of Pomo Indians live in dilapidated modular homes and bungalows.

Almost two-thirds of California voters approved a state constitutional amendment in March 2000 that gave tribes a monopoly to operate big-money casinos in the state. Proposition 1A was touted as a vote for California's long-forgotten Indians—a way to promote economic development and tribal self-reliance, to help pull Native Americans off the welfare rolls, and to redress historic injustices. But as some tribes hatch new plans to build casinos near heavily populated urban areas, voters are second-guessing whether they were snookered.

Four years after California voters gave the green light to Nevada-style casinos on Indian land, signs of a backlash are forming. Some question whether we're barreling too hard and too fast down the one-lane blacktop to Las Vegas.

Rivaling Vegas

"With the Indian tribes, it's almost like the Wild, Wild West," said Nathan Barankin, a spokesman for state Attorney General Bill Lockyer. "The people have seen these businesses go up, and they're no longer just tents. They're big hotels and resorts. And people have had to live for the past four years with traffic issues and the competing demands for natural resources. . . . There's probably a solid majority who still think that we owe the Indians self-sufficiency, but I think what many people are struggling with is, Where do we draw the line for Indian gaming?" As the fast-growing industry takes hold, voters are being asked on Nov. 2 [2004] to decipher complex ballot measures that spin around the issues of whether casinos should be allowed only on Indian land—or also be permitted in card rooms and at racetracks—(Proposition 68) and to what extent casinos should ante-up to the state's treasury and also be held accountable for their impacts on local government services (Proposition 70).[1]

What seemed impossible to imagine only a few years ago, now appears conceivable: In the next decade California could rival Nevada as a mecca for casino gambling resorts. Gambling experts estimate that California's tribal casinos are a $6 billion a year industry (although the tribes claim their revenues are only about half that). Since 1997, the number of slot machines in the state has tripled to about 60,000. Some tribes have already teamed up with major gaming corporations such as Harrah's and Caesars Entertainment to build Las Vegas–style casinos with hotels, spas, and entertainment facilities.

The feds hold most of the face cards. In 1988, Congress passed a sweeping law (the Indian Gaming Regulatory Act) that paved the way for Indian gambling in states that wanted it. Under federal law, if a

---

1. Both Propositions 68 and 70 failed to pass by substantial margins on California's November 2, 2004, ballot.

state allows slot machines and other forms of casino gambling, it must negotiate in good faith with tribes that want to operate casinos. Once a California tribe has land placed in trust by the federal government, the tribe has the right to build a casino on its land. The state's best hope is to collect a portion of the tribes' gambling revenues and to mitigate potential damage to local communities.

California's exposure to Indian gaming is considerable. Fifty-four of the state's 107 federally recognized Indian tribes operate Nevada-style casinos with slot machines; several others have state-tribal compacts but have been slowed by local opposition; and several landless tribes have applied to the federal Bureau of Indian Affairs for grants of restored lands. An additional 54 tribal groups have petitioned for federal recognition—a process that can take decades.

Political Pull

Compared with his predecessor, Gov. Arnold Schwarzenegger seems to want to exercise a firm hand with the tribes. Former Gov. Gray Davis, who accepted nearly $2 million in donations from gaming tribes, negotiated state-tribal compacts with 52 tribes a few months before Prop. 1A was approved. Those compacts left the state with little negotiating leverage to hold the tribes accountable for their casinos' impacts on adjacent communities.

"Tribal casinos are the single most powerful political contributor in California. They give much more than any other special interest," said former Lt. Gov. Leo T. McCarthy, who served on the National Gambling Impact Study Commission. "So they buy a lot of silence with campaign money. There are very few objections to anything they're doing."

Since 1998, California gaming tribes have spent more than $150 million on state legislators, political races and ballot measures. Schwarzenegger has refused to take campaign donations from the tribes.

The public's trepidations about Indian gambling have been inflamed by instances of "reservation shopping" in which landless tribes acquire new land in proximity to population centers, have it put in trust by the U.S. government, and unveil plans to build a casino. Tribal plans to build casinos in Rohnert Park, Richmond, San Pablo, Oakland and unincorporated North Richmond have deeply divided some of these communities.

The fallout has forced politicians to think twice about supporting tribal casinos. Schwarzenegger, who took a lot of flak for his endorsement of the Lytton Band of Pomo Indians' plan to establish an urban casino in San Pablo, is campaigning against Prop. 68 and Prop. 70, measures that could greatly expand the reach of gambling in the state. Opinion polls indicate that both propositions are trailing by huge margins. Racetracks and card clubs behind Prop. 68 decided [in

October 2004] to abandon their campaign, after spending some $25 million on the campaign.

Rep. George Miller, D-Martinez, the author of a 2000 bill to exempt the Lytton Band's development plans from federal and state approvals, said in July [2004] he was surprised to learn of the tribe's desire to replace its San Pablo card club with a six-story casino filled with slot machines.

Broken Promises

Gambling critics accuse some tribes of breaking their promises. Tribal chief Greg Sarris of the Federated Indians of Graton Rancheria testified before Congress in 2000 that his tribe would not build a casino when he sought federal recognition for his tribe—then subsequently announced his tribe's plans to build one in Rohnert Park. Members of the United Auburn Indian Community near Sacramento declared it would not build a casino when it applied for federal recognition, but other tribal members subsequently took power and built the Thunder Valley Casino.

Critics accuse other tribes, which vowed during the Prop. 1A campaign not to expand their casinos, of unveiling elaborate plans for destination resorts soon after the March 2000 election. The 29 Palms Band of Mission Indians in Coachella Valley hooked up with Donald Trump to expand its casino. The Augua Caliente Band of Cahuilla Indians built a second casino near Palm Springs.

"They tell us they're going to build homes or use land for open space, and yet they turn around and develop it into a casino or use it for casino expansion. . . . People get tired of being lied to," said Cheryl Schmit, executive director of Stand Up for California, a nonprofit lobbying group that focuses on tribal gaming. "People are waking up. They realize that Indian gambling does touch them in metropolitan areas. They've heard the horror stories."

George Forman, a San Rafael lawyer who represents the Morongo Band, disputes the notion that the tribes are getting off easy. He notes the Morongo's casino is on a reservation the tribe has occupied since the 1870s.

"The thing you have to remember in looking at California tribes is that these people are survivors of a homegrown holocaust," he said. "That's why you have tribes of relatively small numbers here compared to the Navajo tribe (in Arizona)."

He said that any report of a backlash against Indian casinos is "a gross exaggeration of the number of people and the number of communities where this is a widely held sentiment. . . .

"In most instances, particularly in places where tribes are doing gaming on their own land, this hasn't been a problem. Tribes have made their accommodations with local governments and in most cases their neighbors," he said. "Tribes and local governments are working very well together. The fact that one or two tribes said one thing and did another shouldn't tar all tribes. The same could be said about local planning commissions, board of supervisors and even the governor."

Forman insists that the tribes are increasingly self-sufficient, and paying their way. The Morongo Band maintains its own roads, and operates a health clinic, fire department, police and ambulance services. It has its own water system and sewage treatment system. The Cache Dehe Band of Wintun Indians in Colusa County established a dialysis clinic and wellness center that are both open to the surrounding community. The tribe, which also owns farmlands, has become one of the county's biggest employers.

Mounting Social Costs

But critics say that the most important issues involving the state's foray into big-time gambling have been swept off the table: namely, the societal costs of gambling itself.

Most citizens may be able to occasionally breeze into a casino and drop a tidy sum for an evening's entertainment, but the chronic gambler is trapped in another time zone. Some gamblers spend up to 18 hours a stretch in their favorite casino, take a day or two off, then go back for more.

Most binge bettors cannot afford the game. So, casinos rack up a devastating trail of losses to individuals and their families: bankruptcies, divorces, neglected children, spousal and child abuse, welfare costs and suicides.

"The closer the availability of gambling, especially slot machines for elderly women," McCarthy said, "the more likely you're going to increase the number of gamblers and the number of pathological gamblers."

McCarthy estimates that California has 250,000 "pathological gamblers"—the term used by the American Psychiatric Association to describe chronic gamblers who need professional help. Gambling advocates insist that slot machine addicts comprise only a tiny percentage of casino customers, and that the tribes already contribute to a multi-million-dollar fund to treat gambling addiction. But the state Office of Problem Gambling has not yet been opened.

"I haven't seen any statistics to show that tribal casinos in California have increased the incidence of compulsive gambling," Forman said. "The state already encourages gambling. Most people, to get to a tribal casino, would have to pass several state lottery outlets."

McCarthy has tried for several years to persuade the state Legislature to study gambling's social costs. No such luck.

Those living near casinos also face increased traffic congestion and crime, gambling critics say. Local communities pay for increased police, fire and emergency services; roads to and from casinos; drinking water and sewer improvements; crowded schools; and environmental impacts.

Fighting the Negative Image

The tribes are sensitive to the possibility of a backlash against their casinos. In the 10 gaming compacts tribes have negotiated so far with Schwarzenegger, they have agreed to sit down with local government representatives and assess the fiscal impacts of their casinos on water, power, roads, law enforcement services, problem gambling, schools, environmental and social welfare costs.

One fear from the beginning has been infiltration by organized crime.

"Money does attract crime, but as a general matter, what we've found with respect to traditional organized crime is that Indian tribes have sought to keep it out," said Barankin of the attorney general's office. "We've adopted the Nevada method. By opening up tribal casinos to publicly traded corporations, we've reduced the chance of organized crime getting a foothold in the casinos."

Still, critics say that California's expansion of tribal casinos is a trail of bad choices.

"It's kind of like, Do you want to take poison or shoot yourself in the foot?" said Schmit of Stand Up for California. "People seemed to be accepting of gambling until it was in their backyard. Now that it touches them and the public knows that it will affect them, they're ready to debate the social and economic impacts of gambling."

CHAPTER 3

INTERNET GAMBLING

Contemporary Issues
Companion

INTERNET GAMBLING DAMAGES THE ECONOMY AND HARMS SOCIETY

Ryan D. Hammer

Internet gambling has had a negative impact on the American economy, argues Ryan D. Hammer in the following selection. It deprives state and federal treasuries of tax revenues and takes business away from legal gaming enterprises that do pay taxes, Hammer claims. Since Internet gambling debts are typically paid via credit card, and some gamblers cannot pay their debts, Internet gambling also hurts the creditor and the credit card companies, in Hammer's view. These gambling sites also facilitate problem gambling and underage gambling, Hammer concludes, because of the secluded and anonymous nature of Internet game play. For these reasons, Hammer maintains, lawmakers should continue to fight this illegal industry. Hammer was, at the time of this article's publication, a graduate student in law and business at Indiana University in Bloomington.

The advent of the Internet introduced an entirely new medium for individuals to participate in gambling activities. Unlike traditional land-based casinos, the action at online casinos is perpetual and available to anyone with Internet access. Many online gambling sites operate from locations such as Antigua and Belize, unsupervised by U.S. government regulators. Perhaps the most frightening aspect of Internet gambling is the rampaging growth of the young industry. The Internet gambling explosion poses serious concerns to society.

This [selection] asserts that Internet gambling must be curbed to lessen its negative impact on the American economy. Many state and local governments are dependent on tax revenues associated with traditional forms of gambling. Internet gambling not only deprives the economy of these valuable tax revenues, but also costs the economy valuable jobs and assorted fees associated with traditional gambling. In order to lessen its negative impact on the economy, Internet gambling must be more judiciously regulated in the United States. . . .

Ryan D. Hammer, "Does Internet Gambling Strengthen the U.S. Economy? Don't Bet on It," *Federal Communications Law Journal*, vol. 54, December/January 2001–2002. Copyright © 2001 by the Indiana University School of Law. Reproduced by permission.

Reduction in Tax Revenue

Legal gambling operations in the United States pay millions of dollars in taxes annually to local and federal governments. Without question, these taxes contribute to the overall revenues in the vast majority of states with legalized gambling. "State and local governments in Iowa collected more than $197 million in taxes and fees from Iowa casinos and racetracks [in 2000]." The Casino Queen Riverboat in East St. Louis [Missourri] generates between $10 million and $12 million annually in tax revenues for the city. In addition, the riverboat casino created more than 1,200 full-time jobs. "Gaming revenues have enabled the city to make dramatic strides in its quality of life." The willingness of states to legalize certain forms of gambling, such as lotteries, often hinges on revenue shortfalls of their treasuries. During the 1980s, sixteen of the twenty-two states with the greatest increase in unemployment created lotteries. It is always easier for politicians to support a lottery or a casino riverboat than to propose a tax increase on their constituents.

When Americans participate in Internet gambling, however, no state budget receives a windfall of revenues. The money gambled by Americans on the Internet is done so with companies that pay no taxes in the United States. With over $2 billion gambled on the Internet in 2000, the amount of tax revenues that the United States loses is staggering. Included in this loss of revenues are secondary items purchased when one attends a gambling facility, such as food, souvenirs, and clothing. . . .

While any gambler desires to win money, the depression of losing can be somewhat alleviated when the money is being reinvested to improve the economy. This is the case when people lose money in regulated gambling environments. For example, when an individual buys a lottery ticket at a convenience store, a portion of the cost of that ticket will be used to improve education or to build better roads. When an individual plays an online lottery, the proceeds are not reinvested to improve any government projects. Legal gambling operations are permitted to function in the United States when they comply with strict regulations such as accounting procedures. No such procedures exist in the world of Internet gambling, which deprives the United States of millions of dollars annually in tax revenues.

Consumer Credit Card Industry

Internet gambling places banks and credit card companies in a precarious position. On the one hand, these institutions can profit greatly by offering credit to individuals to gamble online. Credit card charges for Internet gambling are often posted as cash advances, which carry higher interest rates than ordinary purchases. The cash advance rate for most credit cards exceeds 20%. The downside to credit card companies stems from the processing of Internet gambling transactions.

Numerous lawsuits are filed by individuals who have lost money gambling online and who refuse to pay their gambling debts. These lawsuits could leave banks unable to collect debts from individuals who partake in Internet gambling.

As a result of the uncertainty surrounding the litigation of Internet gambling issues, many credit card issuers prohibit transactions from Internet gambling sites. Among the credit card companies that have ceased allowing Internet gambling transactions is Delaware-based MBNA. According to a company spokesman, it "began prohibiting transactions from Internet gambling sites . . . 'when it became apparent how the bank's cards were being used.'" It is expected that other credit card companies will adopt a similar stance to that of MBNA, as the risk of the number of individuals failing to pay their Internet gambling debts increases.

The biggest losers with respect to the use of credit cards in Internet gambling transactions are those who do not gamble online. Regardless of how the litigation evolves in cases of Internet gamblers against credit card companies, the ordinary American loses. If Internet gamblers are successful in having their debts alleviated, non-Internet gamblers will ultimately pay the economic price for their fellow Americans' victory. This price will come in the form of higher fees, charges, and interest rates passed on to all American credit card holders. Because the number of those in the non-Internet gambling community far outweighs the number of those who gamble online, a vast majority of Americans will experience the negative effects of credit card use in Internet gambling transactions.

Even if credit card companies are successful in litigation against Internet gamblers, Americans will still feel negative effects. Victories for credit card companies would provide credibility to the Internet gambling industry and encourage more people to participate. The result of this certification of the Internet gambling industry would cause more and more people to accumulate large Internet gambling debts. When the factor of gambling addiction is added, inevitably many individuals would assume debts unrecoverable to credit card companies. Once again, higher interest rates and fees will be passed on to non-Internet gamblers as a result of the use of credit cards in Internet gambling transactions.

Problem Gambling

The societal concerns that led to the intense regulation of traditional forms of gambling do not disappear when dealing with Internet gambling. As Internet gambling invades American households, society is "left to deal with the crime, bankruptcy, and gambling disorders that may result." Among the many problems exacerbated by Internet gambling are gambling addiction and gambling by minors. Pathological gambling negatively affects not only the gambler, but also the gam-

bler's family and friends, and society at large. Societal costs of pathological gambling includes the expenditure of unemployment benefits,
physical and mental health problems, theft, embezzlement, bankruptcy, suicide, domestic violence, and child abuse and neglect.

Experts predict that "the number of compulsive gamblers could
soon quadruple from 5 million to 20 million addicts nationwide."
The primary reason for this anticipated increase in compulsive gambling is the Internet. With the accessibility of the Internet, gamblers
do not have to travel to casinos or contact their local bookie to place
a bet. Internet gambling is more addictive than other forms of gambling because it combines high-speed, instant gratification with the
anonymity of gambling from home. The temptations that lead to
compulsive gambling are as close as one's computer.

Despite the severe impact that pathological gambling has on Americans, minimal research exists on the topic. The research performed
on pathological gambling has often been half-hearted. An addiction
specialist [Richard C. Leone of the National Gambling Impact Study
Commission] before the House Committee on Banking and Finance
offered the following testimony on pathological gambling:

> [O]ur research indicated that we have a growing number of
> problem and pathological gamblers in America.
>
> We are just beginning to address this problem and calculate
> its costs. The casino industry is supporting limited research,
> but, sadly, it has been difficult to get this matter on the radar
> screen of the major federal funders of research on addictive
> behaviors. . . . In this environment, are we really ready for a
> potentially exponential increase in gambling activity? The
> answer should be obvious.

Compulsive gamblers are responsible for an estimated fifteen percent of the dollars lost in gambling. Beyond this monetary figure,
how can society quantify a divorce caused by a gambling addiction or
a gambling-induced suicide?

Underage Gambling

Another troubling aspect of Internet gambling is the potential access
to minors. Many minors are adept at playing games online and are especially vulnerable to Internet gambling. Whereas state legislation allows casinos to forbid gambling by minors, "Internet gambling eludes
these safeguards." The development of Internet gambling sites has
made wagering even more accessible to minors. In a majority of gambling studies, high school– and college-aged individuals possessed the
highest problem rates. Gambling as a phenomenon among minors is
two to four times more common than among adults. The continued
development of Internet gambling enhances this problem.

Internet gambling sites employ different approaches to prevent minors from participating. The majority of Internet gambling sites utilize credit card information to screen minors because credit is not extended to those under the age of majority. Sites that rely on credit card information, however, alert their company to the possibility that minors will steal credit card information from adults. To prevent this problem, the most sophisticated Internet gambling sites employ credit reporting databases to match credit cards and taxpayer identification numbers to verify the true identities of users. While the number of sites using the matching system is in the minority, this heightened security is a step in the right direction to limit Internet gambling. Regardless, the dangerous combination of minors and gambling is enhanced by the accessibility of Internet gambling sites. . . .

A Need for Action

The Internet gambling industry yields a negative impact on the U.S. economy. Internet gambling deprives state and local governments of valuable tax revenues required to maintain services. Internet gambling also forces consumers to pay higher fees and interest rates as a result of uncollectable gambling debts. Finally, Internet gambling adversely affects our society in ways that cannot easily be quantified such as addiction, pathological behavior, and family disintegration. . . . The negative effects of Internet gambling are already being perceived by the U.S. economy. If lawmakers do not aggressively combat the growth of Internet gambling, the effects on our economy will be damaging.

INTERNET GAMBLING IS A DESTRUCTIVE ADDICTION

Alex Tresniowski et al.

In the following article Alex Tresniowski and other writers for People *magazine report on the fate of online gamblers who have sacrificed time and money to Internet gambling. These gamblers—lured by the ease and privacy of Internet gambling Web sites—claim that they became addicted to this type of wagering, the authors write. Some ruined their credit ratings by running up huge debts on credit cards; others took to theft and embezzlement to pay off their debts. Even more disturbing, the authors note, is that the anonymous nature of Internet gambling has enticed many minors to place bets, often leading them into the trap of problem gambling at an early age.*

They would wait patiently for night, tuck their two kids into bed and, in the privacy of their study, give in to their demons. For a nightmarish six months [in 2002], Andy and Lisa Harding, solid middle-class parents from Dublin, Calif., logged on to gambling Web sites and played slots, blackjack, craps and roulette late into the night, clicking away their savings and nearly sinking their family. "Soon I started gambling more than we were earning," says Lisa, 39, a retail store manager. "You don't realize what you're spending—betting is so easy."

The Hardings quickly ran up more than $100,000 in gambling debts, stopping only after they had maxed out their credit cards. Soon after, a bank that issued one of the credit cards sued them. Deviant as their dead-of-night sprees may seem, the Hardings are far from alone in their addiction. Since gambling's Internet debut in 1995 the number of Web sites offering round-the-clock gaming has risen from a handful to nearly 2,000, with the industry expected to rake in as much as $6 billion worldwide [in 2003]. According to a 2002 University of Connecticut study, at least 8 percent of those surveyed have gambled online; of them, 74 percent are believed to have a serious problem. "It's high-speed, flashy, alluring and promises something for nothing," says Angie Moore, manager of the Illinois Institute for Addiction Recovery. "Those are ingredients that lead to addictive behavior." Says Don Hulen, executive director of the Arizona Council on Compulsive Gambling: "You can't detect it the way you can detect alcoholics, yet compulsive gambling on the Internet can destroy lives as surely as any drug."

Privacy and Unrestricted Access

Like Internet porn, online gambling hooks users by offering unprecedented access and privacy. "You can bet in your own home, in your pajamas, 24 hours a day," says Andy Harding, 42, a sheet metal worker who occasionally visited casinos before joining his wife in betting online. While gambling anywhere but in legitimate venues is illegal in the U.S., the companies running gambling Web sites are based outside the country, which lets them skirt the law and solicit business here with tempting pop-up ads. Lisa Harding clicked on one such ad in March 2002, and at first bet only for fun. "Whenever I hit a jackpot, a message kept flashing: 'Play for real! You could win real money!'" she says. "So I started betting with my credit card."

And it was oh so easy. All an online gambler has to do is type in a credit card number in order to instantly receive virtual chips. (The Hardings have brought a suit against their debtors, including Visa and MasterCard, claiming they violated state laws by handling betting transactions.) Operating almost entirely without regulation, the sites have made Internet gambling "an activity that preys on children, is rife with fraud and aids money laundering," claims Sen. Jon Kyl (R-Ariz.), who has a pending bill that would ban credit card companies from accepting charges for such gaming. "It ruins credit ratings and allows young people to build up thousands of dollars in debts on their parents' cards."

Enticing Minors

In fact, few sites have any effective mechanisms to block minors from gambling. One recent national survey of 14- to 22-year-olds by the University of Pennsylvania's Institute for Adolescent Risk Communication found that 11 percent of males admitted to gambling online, up dramatically from just a few years earlier. "A lot of the Internet gambling Web sites entice you in like a video game, so the whole format is really seductive to kids," says George Meldrum, director of special projects at the Delaware Council on Gambling Problems. "And the earlier the onset of an activity, the more likely you are to become addicted."

Take the case of John, who was only 12 when he gambled for the first time, wagering on himself in a golf match. But his gambling only became a major problem 11 years later, after he switched to online betting in his apartment while at the University of Utah. "I bet every day for two years and gambled away all my tuition money," says the banking officer, now 26, who does not want his real name used. "Basically, I was out of control." He lost about $40,000, somehow graduated from college and seven months later joined Gamblers Anonymous.

A Secret Addiction

Traditionally, around 95 percent of people who seek treatment for gambling problems are men. But since the advent of online gambling, experts have seen a spike in the number of women looking for help. "Now the numbers are closer to 40 percent women," says Nancy Petry, an associate professor of psychiatry at the University of Connecticut Health Center and a researcher for the 2002 study. "Typically, women are seeking relief from boredom and loneliness. And the betting is all on their credit card so they don't see the damage until a month later."

Fredia Mendick, 53, knew all about that damage long before she discovered online gambling. Convicted of embezzling $120,000 from her former employer, an attorney, to pay for her casino gambling habit in the late '80s and early '90s, she served 14 months in prison. After that she managed not to gamble for nine years—until she clicked on a pop-up ad in 2000 and got sucked right back in. "It got so I could hardly wait for my husband to go to work," says Mendick. "I played keno all day until he came home." Finally, three months later, Mike Mendick, 60, a computer administrator in Phoenix, noticed $11,000 was missing from their bank account. He came home early one day to investigate—and surprised his wife gambling online. "I was furious," he says. "Any safety net we had built up was gone and our credit rating went to hell."

Mike persuaded his wife to enter therapy and dismantled their computer. Today the terminal is back in the living room of the couple's home in Avondale, a Phoenix suburb. Every once in a while, a gambling ad pops up while Fredia is online, "but I just know that I can't do it," she says. "It's so easy that, to sick people like me, it's destructive. It destroys families."

Not Just a Game

Andy and Lisa Harding flirted with just such a fate. At first they hid their online gambling from their two sons, now 14 and 6. Soon the children caught on, but thought it was just a game. Just before the Hardings were sued, the truth emerged. "It took its toll on our boys for them to see us so stressed and upset," says Lisa.

While they await hearings on the lawsuits, the Hardings are dealing with their devastated credit—and their deep shame. "I think about our life before, and I wonder how things got so bad so quick," says Andy. "I put my family in danger. Who knows what's going to happen?" That, he surely realizes now, is anyone's bet.

Internet Sports Betting Is a Serious Problem

Tom Weir

USA Today sportswriter Tom Weir states in the following article that online sports betting is a growing attraction. As Weir's investigation reveals, online sports betting is addictive for many gamblers and typically entices college-educated men who have participated in sports during their youth. Weir also reports that many current athletes are also victims of compulsive Internet sports betting. Particularly troubling, Weir contends, is that some of these athletes are college players who have bet on the outcomes of their own games or even taken money to perform poorly in order to alter the online odds.

A college senior sits at his laptop. His wife is in another room, thinking her husband is writing a term paper. Instead he's on an Internet gambling Web site, where he's able to bet on virtually any professional or college sports event by charging the wagers to a credit card. His losses have reached $25,000. His tuition money is gone. And he can't stop.

That's how one Internet gambling addict described his predicament recently to Arnie Wexler, who runs a national hotline for problem gamblers.

Wexler, who promises confidentiality to callers, is among the counselors dealing with a rapid increase in gambling addictions in teenagers and college students. They blame the addictive behavior on the growing accessibility of gambling Web sites—25 in 1997, roughly 1,800 [in 2003].

"Internet gambling is probably the most dangerous thing we've got going at this time," Wexler says. "It's available 24 hours a day. You can do it in your pajamas or your birthday suit."

No one can be certain just how big the industry has become, but government officials and industry insiders estimate overall losses on Internet gambling among Americans will amount to more than $3 billion [in 2003].

In Congress, where some members are concerned about the explosion of Internet gambling and the possibility that athletes might be betting on their own games, moves are underway to curb the industry. Some industry officials insist Internet gambling is so big it cannot be stopped.

Internet gambling is illegal in the USA but is permitted to operate in numerous other nations. Most of the Web sites operate out of the Caribbean or Latin America but are accessible anywhere in the world.

"You'd be shocked at how many kids are doing this," says Ed Looney, director of the New Jersey Council on Compulsive Gambling. "The No. 1 form of problem gambling for college students is Internet betting on sports."

At the Algamus Recovery Center in Anna Maria, Fla., director Rick Benson says the treatment facility for gambling addicts has seen a 25% increase in Internet-related cases [since 2001]. Benson says the majority are white, college-educated males, "with some high level of competitive sports participation in their background."

A Problem for Pro Athletes

Internet gambling traps well-known individuals, too. In June [2003], Washington Capitals hockey star Jaromir Jagr admitted he ran up a $500,000 debt betting on sports events five years ago with the Belize-based CaribSports Web site.

Former Florida State quarterback Adrian McPherson pleaded no-contest [in July 2003] to misdemeanor charges of betting on college and professional sports, including his own games, on the Costa Rica–based site SBG Global. He was sentenced to community service but received no jail time and is hopeful the NCAA [National Collegiate Athletic Association] will let him play again. [In August 2003] he enrolled at Tennessee State.

Such cases show how "Internet gambling is going to become an increasing problem with athletes," says U.S. Sen. Jon Kyl, R-Ariz., sponsor of legislation that would make it illegal for U.S. banks and all other financial institutions to transfer funds to gambling Web sites.

"I do think it represents a relatively new threat to the integrity of sport, because of the younger generation growing up with computers," Kyl says. "It's just a natural part of their life and (shows) the ease with which they're exposed to gambling on the Internet."

The Senate Banking Committee approved his bill unanimously July 31 [2003]. In June the House passed a similar bill 319-104. Such legislation has been approved by both houses before but never in the same year. Kyl's bill goes to the full Senate for a vote.

Industry insiders say that instead of prohibiting Internet gambling, Congress could be generating millions in revenue for the USA if only the enterprise were taxed.

"The sad fact is that we have members of Congress who not only are in the dark about the realities of Internet gambling, they want to put their heads further in the sand," says Alan Feldman, spokesman for the MGM Mirage casino, which has shut down its offshore gambling Web site because of congressional opposition.

Easy Access for Minors

The growing concern is online gambling may create more addicts.

It's very easy for a young person to take a parent's credit or debit card and open an account to bet online. The Federal Trade Commission [in 2002] reported an informal survey of 100 gambling Web sites found young people could gain easy access, that warnings on underage gambling generally were hard to find and that 20% of the Web sites had no warnings.

Internet gambling is "so new that even if there were a whole bunch of pathological (Internet) gamblers, we wouldn't know about them," says Christine Reilly of Harvard University's Institute for Research on Pathological Gambling and Related Disorders.

A 2001 study by the Harvard institute suggests young computer users have an increased risk of becoming problem gamblers. The study found that 5% to 6% of college-age and younger people are "pathological" in their betting—gambling to recoup losses, spending money they don't have, unable to stop—compared with 1% to 2% of the general population. . . .

"There's not a lot of awareness of it," Reilly says. "If clinicians would just become aware and start screening, we could probably head off (many) problems. The focus has been on drugs and alcohol."

That same unknowing attitude is prevalent among young Internet gamblers, says Pat Fowler, executive director of the Florida Council on Compulsive Gambling.

"A lot don't even realize it's illegal to do it," Fowler says of the rarely prosecuted crime of sports betting, legal only in Nevada. "They go into it thinking that, because it's available on the Internet, it must be legal. It tends to be the primary source of wagering for college students, especially for sports wagers. [Online] they don't have the fear of placing bets with a bookie, which most know is illegal."

Of the nearly 7,000 callers to the helpline of Fowler's organization last year, 7% from all age groups said their gambling debts were $175,000 or more, presumably including Internet gambling. Identification of people with Internet gambling problems is so new, there aren't many statistics solely pertaining to that form of betting.

Student Athletes Involved

The secrecy and accessibility of Internet gambling also make it easier for athletes to gamble on events they participate in. The NCAA hopes to complete by early [2004] a survey of 30,000 college athletes on gambling issues. Bill Saum, the NCAA's director of gambling activities, says he's certain it will show student-athlete betting has increased since two other often-cited studies were done:

- In 1998, a University of Michigan study found 35% of 758 student-athletes surveyed had gambled on sports and that 5% of the males had either provided inside information for gambling purposes, bet on their own games or accepted money to play poorly.
- In 2000 a University of Cincinnati study found 25.5% of the 648 Division I basketball and football players surveyed had gambled on college sports events, 3.7% on their games, and 0.5% had accepted money to play poorly.

Legislation to Curb Internet Gambling

For those who contend Internet gambling has become too widespread to stop, Saum says the pending congressional legislation "is a good first step."

"Just because something is difficult to stop is (not) a reason to give in," he says. "The more roadblocks we put up, the more it will help."

Legislation to block payments to online gambling operations has been supported by all U.S. major pro sports leagues and the NCAA.

"To do anything to constrain gambling is really, really difficult," says U.S. Rep. Jim Leach, R-Iowa, who has proposed several bills to curb Internet gambling.

"When I first introduced the legislation three or four years ago [in 2000], the credit card companies were massively opposed. As time has gone on, they have figured out they are the losers. Even though they were making tidy sums in transactions, when people can't pay back their transactions, the credit card companies have to pick it up.". . .

American Express has a long-standing policy against allowing gambling charges, and Visa has begun regular audits to guard against "7995" purchases, the credit card code for gambling transactions.

Initially, the voluntary crackdown by credit card companies "had a huge impact," says Sebastian Sinclair, president of Maine-based Christiansen Capital Advisors, a gambling consultant company that tracks Internet wagering. . . .

But he says voluntary stoppage by U.S. credit card companies actually has worked for the Internet gambling operators, giving them time to set up payment methods that will be more difficult if not impossible for Congress to restrict.

It appears bettors might be able to outflank any action by Congress. Sinclair says bettors often use bank debit cards or wire transfers. If those means of transferring funds are outlawed by Congress, most gambling Web sites provide links to overseas companies such as ClearPay and NETeller for bettors to set up "e-wallets." Another option not covered by the legislation is TeleBuy, which puts gambling charges on the bettor's phone bill.

Sinclair estimates Internet gambling losses at about $6 billion worldwide [in 2003]. In 1997, he says, it was about $300 million.

The Price of Prohibition

Given the rapid increase, the Internet gambling industry says Congress would be wiser to legalize, regulate and tax their business, as Australia, New Zealand and the United Kingdom have done. . . .

Sportingbet founder Mark Blandford estimates that if his $70 million in online wagers from U.S. bettors were taxed at the same rate as Las Vegas casinos, he'd owe the government $4.4 million this year. "We'd happily pay it if we could come into a regulated market," says Blandford, whose Web site is available in nine languages.

Kyl's reply: "We're not in this to make money. We're in this to maintain the integrity of sports."

Since U.S. credit card companies stopped processing gambling transactions, Blandford says, "It hasn't made a material difference."

Blandford's prediction? "You're going to see players setting up non-American bank accounts. The genuine prohibitionists are going to create a money-laundering environment. It's a huge industry. You can't turn back the clock."

Banning Internet Gambling Sets a Dangerous Precedent

David G. Schwartz

David G. Schwartz is a professor and coordinator of the Gaming Studies Research Center at the University of Nevada, Las Vegas. In the following article Schwartz acknowledges that operators of land-based casinos, also known as "terrestrial casinos," might reasonably be opposed to Internet gambling. As Schwartz points out, some in the terrestrial casino industry view Internet casinos as unwanted and unregulated competition. However, he suggests that if these operators tolerate the government's prohibition of Internet gambling, they might in time find their land-based casinos the target of similar prohibition laws.

The Internet, something that most people never knew they needed, has become [since the early 1990s] a seemingly essential part of everyday life and business. Without the unfettered access to information, entertainment, and instant communication that the Internet provides, life would be profoundly slower, and only the most terminally nostalgic of Luddites would propose dismantling the electronic information highway. Yet the Internet has also brought challenges to the status quo, and one of the most provocative has been the growth of online gambling. The question of whether online wagering should be permitted, though, reaches far beyond ISPs [Internet service providers] and payment providers, because it has serious implications for anyone connected to the gaming business. By enacting laws against Internet gambling, state and federal governments may come perilously close to circumscribing one of the freedoms that has historically driven the American economy and allowed for the unparalleled growth of the casino entertainment industry—consumer choice. If Congress has the right to ban Americans from choosing to wager on the Internet, it is certainly conceivable that the federal government can bar Americans from gambling anywhere. For the gaming industry, a federal ban on Internet gambling is a bad idea.

David G. Schwartz, "A Virtual Pandora's Box: What Cyberspace Gambling Prohibition Means to Terrestrial Casino Operators," *UNLV Gaming Research & Review Journal*, vol. 7, 2003, pp. 59–64. Copyright © 2003 by the International Gaming Institute. Reproduced by permission.

The Growth of Online Wagering

Internet gambling has had a brief, explosive, though not entirely unprecedented, history. Throughout recorded history, one thing has remained constant—with technical or social innovations will come new kinds of gambling. This is clearly seen in the history of American gambling. The rise of riverboat travel in the 1830s, for example, facilitated the creation of that most mythical of American characters, the riverboat gambler. The advent of affordable auto and air travel, of course, made possible the creation of a national gambling vacation destination on the Las Vegas Strip. Similarly, it was not long before enterprising operators realized that the real-time communication offered by the Internet created the possibility for a virtual casino.

Today, Internet gambling is booming, despite its ostensible criminal status in the United States. Since the appearance of the first online wagering site, Internet casinos have become an accepted dimension of cyberspace. By 2001, there were well over 1400 domain names for online gaming sites and about 300 providers—businesses and governments that actually run these wagering sites. More than 60 jurisdictions had, by that year, decided to license, regulate, or endorse Internet gaming [according to S. Schneider in the *Internet Gambling Report V* (2002)].

Pundits feel that in the near future the online gaming industry will see a degree of consolidation and maturation similar to that of other new industries after an initial wide-open pioneering phase. Should Internet gambling receive the imprimatur of a federally-sanctioned state regulatory body within the United States, industry observers expect to see an even more rapid consolidation, if American consumers opt to wager at licensed, regulated, reputable sites backed by major terrestrial [land-based] casino operators. Instead of the 300+ operators currently offering online wagering, perhaps 50 or so groups will host cyber casinos. This is, not coincidentally, a process that has been seen in the terrestrial casino industry for about the past fifty years—as early as 1958, a *Newsweek* article declared that "the day of the small gambler is over," as large combines could better balance profit and risk. Today, large corporations dominate the commercial casino market, and it seems reasonable that the same process will happen in cyberspace.

The Urge to Ban Internet Gambling

On the surface, a state-taxed, regulated business operated by respected, known companies seems desirable for all concerned. The chief obstacle to this rational, ordered state of affairs is a lingering resistance to the idea of American regulation of Internet gambling, and the belief that the federal government should in fact prosecute those who offer online gambling. This opposition comes from many quarters: shortsighted terrestrial operators, those opposed to any expansion of gambling or specifically Internet gambling, and well-meaning citizens who are simply uninformed.

Terrestrial operators who oppose the regulation of Internet gambling, on the face of it, seem to be acting from rational self-preservation. After all, how is a casino with hundreds of millions of dollars sunk into its physical plant, to say nothing of a payroll of several thousand employees, supposed to compete with an online casino that has a fraction of those costs? If convenience were the ultimate indicator of gambling choice, terrestrial casinos, at best a car or plane trip away, would be necessarily put out of business by in-home Internet casinos. Some operators fear that disreputable online casinos will taint the integrity that the commercial casino industry has struggled to build, and that public anger against fly-by-night operators of online casinos might feed a more inchoate anti-gambling mood. Those who make their living from regulated, taxed terrestrial casinos, in this argument, have nothing to gain and much to lose from Internet competitors.

Then there are those who oppose, on grounds of principle or expedience, any expansion of gambling. For these, the proliferation of Internet gambling has seen the gnashing of teeth as, powerless, they watch Americans choose to gamble in their own homes. Gambling opponents see Internet gambling as the final line in the sand for gambling operators to cross—if opposition to gambling fails here, there will be no place that Americans are "protected" from gambling.

Others favor gambling in casinos, but specifically oppose online wagering because of the new problems it raises. The authors of H.R. 556, the [James A.] Leach-[John] LaFalce Internet Gambling Enforcement Act, concluded that Internet gambling was a "major cause of debt collection problems" for banks and credit card companies, and that offshore Internet casinos presented "a significant money laundering vulnerability" (House of Representatives, 2002). While they felt that the terrestrial industry could control money laundering, they saw unregulated online casinos as impossible to control.

Most opponents of Internet gambling, though, don't fall into either of these categories. They are simply disinterested observers who have concluded that Internet gambling is a bad idea. In an article in the *Federal Communications Law Review*, [Ryan] Hammer (2001) summarized three elements of this position. First, the proliferation of Internet gambling will inevitably lead to a loss of tax revenue, as Americans choose to gamble at untaxed Internet casinos instead of taxed terrestrial ones. Second, credit card companies who allow online-gambling transactions run the risk of lawsuits by customers seeking to avoid payment of their gambling debts—the costs of any litigation, and of fees alleviated, are passed on to other customers in the form of higher interest rates and fees. Finally, there are a host of other miscellaneous costs that cannot be quantified but nonetheless present compelling reasons to stop online wagering: pathological gambling, increased bankruptcies, and a nebulous array of social problems long associated with gambling.

These well-meaning arguments against Internet gambling are troubling for three reasons. First, they assume that Internet gambling will strip revenue from the commercial casino industry, which is taxed, and that states will thus lose a portion of their revenues. Second, this position assumes that online wagering will always be unregulated and untaxed in the United States. Should the regulatory and legal framework of Internet gambling in the United States be codified, most of the first two arguments against online wagering (loss of taxes and credit card liabilities) will be rendered moot. Third, and more importantly for terrestrial operators, the "costs to society" argument can be made just as persuasively against terrestrial casinos. For that matter, invoking "miscellaneous costs to society" as justification for legal prohibition can, logically, lead to the federal banning of smoking, drinking alcohol to excess, gorging on fast food, or driving while talking on a cellular phone. Followed through to their logical extremes, arguments to prohibit Internet gambling via federal statute are less than compelling.

Despite the specious nature of anti-Internet gambling arguments, federal legislators and law enforcement agencies have devoted a significant amount of time and taxpayer money attempting to throttle online wagering. Net gambling foes cite the 1961 Wire Act as ample justification for federal action. This law, originally intended to squelch the transmission of racing and betting information over the telephone and telegraph, makes illegal the use of a "wire communication facility" to transmit bets or wagering information across state or national borders. Since most Internet Service Providers use telephone or cable lines, the official position of the United States government is that those who offer gambling over the Internet are breaking the law.

Internet Prohibition: The Wrong Choice

If the intentions of the Wire Act's framers count for anything, it is worth noting that, they would likely approve of applying the Wire Act to Internet gambling. After all, the Internet is nothing but another "wire communication facility," albeit one with far more sophistication than a bookie sitting by a rotary-dial phone. In 1961, Congress did what it could to halt the spread of gambling. While not attacking gambling within the states (a violation of states' rights it dared not attempt), it clearly said that gambling, besides established exceptions for off-track betting, cannot cross state lines. Until specifically changed by statute, that remains the letter—and spirit—of the federal law.

But the United States, specifically in regard to gambling, is hardly the same place it was in 1961, when only Nevada had legal casino gambling. New Hampshire's state lottery, which would open the door for the revival of state-sanctioned gambling, was still three years off. [In 2003], forty-eight states have some form of legal gambling, and no less than eleven states actively regulate commercial casinos. It is hard to drive more than a few hours in any direction without finding some kind of gambling facility. Most Americans would be hard pressed to go about their daily routines without passing a chance to gamble since convenience stores sell lottery tickets in most states, and bingo halls dot the American landscape. Simply put, Americans have legalized—and legitimized—their long-standing predilection towards gambling. It is now states that prohibit gambling that are exceptional. Clearly, Americans no longer agree with the framers of the Wire Act, and feel that gambling is better served by regulation than prohibition.

Still, some in Congress have seized the anti-gambling banner. The first attempt to specifically target Internet gambling, Senator Jon Kyl's 1997 Internet Gambling Prohibition Act, would have criminalized the act of betting over the Internet by penalizing both online casinos and online bettors. Though this act passed the Senate, the House of Representatives never voted on a parallel bill. Senator Kyl amended the bill in 1999 to punish only those who offered online gambling with fines and prison sentences. Once again, the bill passed the Senate, but a similar bill failed in the House. Thus, the American people escaped the 20th century with no new laws against online gambling.

But in October 2002, the House passed by voice vote the Leach-Lafalce Internet Gambling Enforcement Act, which would prohibit the use of "bank instruments" (credit cards, debit cards, and wire transfers) in Internet gambling. As of this article's writing, it had been referred to the Senate but had not yet been voted on. The White House, however, urged Senate Majority Leader Tom Daschle to act on the bill, noting that Internet gambling had caused "countless heartbreaking stories" of personal ruin, and that the unregulated industry served as a haven for money launderers and terrorists. Congressman Michael Oxley has gone even further, stating that the Internet Gambling Enforcement Act is "just as essential to American families as homeland security and terrorism insurance" [as related in R. Smith's article for the *Las Vegas Review-Journal*]. Clearly, there are those who believe that online wagering is as inimical a threat as any that the United States faces. This rhetoric, while heated, has not carried over into definitive legislative action against online gambling, but there is no reason to believe that it will not.[1]

Should the opponents of Internet gambling regulation carry the day, Americans will be officially prohibited from wagering on the Internet. Companies that "permit" American citizens to do so will be subject to prosecution, and those who advertise or facilitate payment for Internet gambling sites licensed by other jurisdictions but "illegal" in the United States will also be liable to criminal penalties. It will be illegal for credit card companies to process online wagering transac-

1. As of this writing, no action has been taken on this bill, which remains in the Senate Judiciary Committee.

tions. Americans will, effectively, be denied any choice in the matter of gambling online, on paper. Of course, this will probably not prevent millions of Internet users from gambling, but Congress will have acted to the best of its ability. . . .

There is little to suggest that Congress should have the power to ban activities that are legal in the majority of states. Most Americans can hardly avoid the opportunities for legal, state-sanctioned gambling, be they at casinos, racetracks, or in convenience stores, which sell lottery tickets. Given the variety of problems facing law enforcement at every level, it seems misguided to funnel human resources into policing online gambling when gambling is already readily available to most Americans.

Internet gambling prohibition has many implications that go beyond the right to bet online. Should the federal government implement a ban on online wagering, it will set a dangerous precedent for cyberspace, for the U.S. Congress will have taken the right to say what are and are not appropriate uses of Internet commerce. Even if the American people voted with unanimity to ban Internet gambling, how could the United States force the Netherlands Antilles—or Australia—to prevent their regulated online gaming industries from accepting bets from American consumers? . . .

The Implications for Terrestrial Operators

Thus, federal efforts to prohibit Internet gambling are simply not workable. There is no reason to believe that communications technology will stand still while the federal government devises a system to stop Americans from gambling online. While American jurisdictions are powerless against online casinos, they exercise very real authorities over land-based commercial casinos, and these operators might be haunted by efforts to ban online gambling.

Should the federal government be somehow granted the right and power to deny Americans the ability to wager online, there is little logical reason to stop there. After all, if gambling is a socially undesirable activity, why should gambling businesses be allowed to advertise over the Internet? Isn't a website that displays a banner ad for a Las Vegas casino encouraging its visitors to gamble, or facilitating a gambling transaction? How about casino web sites? Even though they may not allow visitors to bet online, they do provide prospective patrons with information about their casinos, which is no doubt facilitating future gambling transactions. What about sites that allow travelers to make reservations at casino hotels? Though they are not gambling, they are arranging to stay at an establishment with gambling, and they are also directly supporting a "gambling business."

Terrestrial casino operators, then, should not be drawn in by chimerical hopes of using federal Internet gambling prohibition to stifle a potential rival industry. When put it its most basic form, the question of Internet gambling becomes one of consumer choice—should citizens have the right to decide how they want to spend their money, or should the federal government choose how they can do so?

If terrestrial casino operators truly want to shore up their defenses against losses to online casinos, they must offer a more appealing product. The world's gambling capital, Las Vegas, rose to prominence precisely because it offered visitors a mix of casino action, entertainment, and vacation pleasures. Casinos throughout the nation may have to re-invent themselves as all-inclusive entertainment destinations that have more than just nickel slot machines. Or they might need to get back to increasing the appreciation of the gambling experience itself. One of the attractions of a night of gambling is the public, theatrical element; it is hard to believe that people will give up the shared excitement of a hot blackjack table for the cold reality of a solitary point-and-click wagering experience.

PROHIBITING INTERNET GAMBLING IS IMPOSSIBLE

Tom W. Bell

In the following article law professor Tom W. Bell observes that Internet gambling has attracted many vocal opponents—from land-based casino owners to federal and state politicians. Internet gambling sites are competing for the same patrons that play state lotteries or frequent land-based casinos, Bell writes. However, in spite of prohibitionary legislation, the government has not succeeded in staunching the public's interest in Internet gambling, nor has it effectively closed down gambling Web sites, which are primarily operated from foreign countries. Internet technology coupled with the limits of U.S. jurisdiction make banning Internet gambling impossible, Bell argues. In fact, he maintains, the government will soon realize that it is not even desirable to keep such a ban in place once the government figures out how to regulate and profit from legalizing the Internet gambling industry. Bell, who teaches at Chapman University Law School in California, is a member of the Cato Institute, a libertarian public policy foundation.

When Angel—mother, wife, and self-described "patriotic Italian-American"—feels like unwinding, she heads to the bingo parlor. But Angel (not her real name) avoids the local church's game: She doesn't like the smoke, and besides, "The crowd can get pretty vicious at Immaculate Mary's when the callers are inadequate."

Nor does she fly to Atlantic City or Las Vegas. "I'm not against that personally," she explains on her Web site. "The coffee boys in Caesar's are very buff. They can serve me in their little togas anytime. But road trips don't go over real well when you're a Mommy. You sorta hafta stay home and take care of things, capice?"

For Angel, the nearest bingo parlor waits on just the other side of an Internet connection. Like an increasing number of Americans, she loves the convenience and fun of online gaming. "If I choose to be a

Tom W. Bell, "Gambler's Web: Online Betting Can't Be Stopped—and Why Washington Shouldn't Bother Trying," *Reason*, October 1, 1999. Copyright © 1999 by the Reason Foundation, 3415 S. Sepulveda Blvd., Suite 400, Los Angeles, CA 90034, www.reason.com. Reproduced by permission.

chooch [slang for one who lacks common sense or is hardheaded] and spend my money here unwisely, it's my choice," she writes. But if a potent coalition of lobbyists and politicians gets its way, neither Angel nor any other American will have the legal right to make that choice.

Though it defies exact measurement, all studies of the Internet gambling market agree that it's growing explosively. It more than doubled from 1997 to 1998, according [to] a widely cited report by economist Sebastian Sinclair, with the number of gamblers increasing from 6.9 million to 14.5 million and revenue jumping from $300 million to $651 million. By 2001, Sinclair predicts, 43 million Internet gamblers will generate $2.3 billion in revenue. Estimates of the number of gaming Web sites vary from 250 to 1,000, ranging from online casinos to sports betting sites to lotteries, tournaments, bingo games, and sweepstakes.

The Motives of Prohibitionists

Not surprisingly, the old boys' network of licensed, land-based gambling businesses does not welcome competition from this worldwide digital network. They aren't losing much money to it yet. But they will soon, and they know it.

So do their political patrons. Politicians relish the taxes that pour in from tightly regulated casinos, parimutuel tracks, and similar operations—some $3.7 billion in 1997. Net gambling, by contrast, pays virtually no taxes.

What's more, the government itself owns a share of the gambling market, with 37 states and the District of Columbia sponsoring lotteries. Those lottos earned $14.9 billion in 1997, in part by offering the worst odds of any common form of gambling. They consequently have the most to fear from online competition.

The gaming industry helps politicians fight off another sort of competitor: candidates who campaign against them. The industry's federal campaign contributions increased 447 percent during the 1990s. Its soft money and PAC [political action committees] contributions hit nearly $6.3 million in the 1997–98 election cycle, more than double the $2.6 million it gave in the previous nonpresidential cycle. It spent even more at the state level, the locus of most U.S. gambling policy, giving more than $100 million in donations and lobbying fees to state legislators from 1992 to 1996.

Unsurprisingly, some politicians want to restrict Internet gambling. Sen. Jon Kyl (R-Ariz.) claims that online gaming lets you "click the mouse and bet the house." His response—the Internet Gambling Prohibition Act of 1999, whose penalties include fines of up to $20,000 and four years in prison—would send a different message: "Use e-mail and go to jail."

By their plain language, several federal statutes already outlaw Internet gambling. The Federal Interstate Wire Act prohibits using interstate communications to run a gambling business. The Organized Crime Control Act of 1970 makes it a federal crime to engage in a gambling business illegal under state law. The federal Travel Act, as read broadly by the courts, criminalizes all interstate communications meant to facilitate the distribution of gambling proceeds. If Net gambling is unhindered nonetheless, this suggests not that the police lack the authority to stop it but that they lack the interest—or ability.

In essence, Kyl's law would make it illegal to send or receive bets using an interactive computer service. He misrepresents the bill as a mere update of the Wire Act. In fact, it targets online gaming for new and special penalties. It would expand the definition of a "gambling business" to include anyone who wins more than $2,000 in a day. It would also, unlike the Wire Act, make it a federal crime to gamble to and from states that have legalized the games in question. And whereas the Wire Act modestly limits its scope to transmissions "in interstate or foreign commerce," Kyl's bill targets any messages sent over a computer service connected to the Internet. It would thus cover e-mail sent across town, or even across the hall.

An earlier version of the act passed the Senate 90-10 [in 1998], only to expire in the House when the clock ran out on the 105th Congress. This time, the prospects for passage look good.[1] Kyl can cite support from both Republicans and Democrats, from state, local, and federal law enforcement, and from private groups ranging from the Christian Coalition to Ralph Nader's Public Citizen.

It's a funny bill, filled with telling loopholes. Kyl says he's targeting gambling because it "erodes the values of hard work, sacrifice, and personal responsibility." Yet his proposal aims selectively at those who would compete with the existing gaming industry. State lotteries, duly licensed parimutuel race tracks, and the booming fantasy sports business win broad exemptions under the bill. Casinos benefit, too, both because they participate in parimutuel betting networks and because their Megabuck shared-payoff slot machine network falls within the bill's loopholes. Even the Department of Justice criticized Kyl's bill for treating segments of the incumbent industry too favorably, arguing that "there are no legitimate reasons why these gambling operations should be exempted from the ban while other forms of gambling are not."

In June [1999], Sen. Dianne Feinstein (D-Calif.), a co-sponsor of the bill, offered a candid explanation for the exemptions. Notwithstanding the bill's stated aim, she testified, "it became very clear that there were some legitimate interests that also needed some recognition, and so the bill does contain provisions for horse racing." A lobbying free-for-all apparently followed. "Now, the problem is that once that was done others wanted into it, and the bill contains a similar exception

---

1. Similar bills have been introduced in the House (H.R.2143) and the Senate (S.627), but as of this writing neither has passed.

for dog racing, which is also dependent on wagering. Other modifications have been made to the legislation, making certain that legal fantasy sports leagues can continue to operate, and that an important source of revenue for state lotteries [is] not disrupted."

Cutting Out the Competition

A similar odor of special interest dealing hovers around the National Gambling Impact Study Commission, whose final report—mandated by Congress and published [in] June [1999]—wails that "millions of families throughout the nation suffer from the effects of problem and pathological gambling," including "depression, abuse, divorce, homelessness, and suicide." Since no modern political statement is complete without an invocation of "the children," the commission duly links underage gaming to alcohol and drug abuse, violent behavior, truancy, and low grades.

And what powerful, sweeping remedy does the commission propose to stop such woes? A moratorium on the expansion of gambling.

The incumbent industry must have raised many a toast to that recommendation. Though already well-protected from competition by highly restrictive licensing schemes, it would, if the commission's proposal became law, win a legal lock on the gaming market. Its would-be competitors online, not having jumped through the requisite regulatory hoops, would never even get started.

In the short run, then, Kyl's bill will mean trouble for the fledgling industry, its customers, and the Internet service providers (ISPs) who connect them. But it will not stop online gambling. The very architecture of the Internet will frustrate prohibition.

The Impossibility of Regulation

The Internet relies on a packet switching protocol that breaks each message into discrete parts and sends them over various unpredictable routes, to be reassembled at the message's destination. It's a bit like writing a letter, chopping it up, and mailing each piece separately to the same address.

Now imagine Congress ordering the U.S. Postal Service to search for and seize all correspondence related to illegal gambling. The post office would object to the cost and futility of the task, while its customers would object to having their privacy violated. Nor could the postmen simply stop delivering mail to and from addresses associated with illegal gambling. Gamblers would simply change their P.O. boxes periodically and send letters without return addresses.

Attempts to ban Internet gambling face even higher hurdles. The flood of data alone prevents ISPs from discriminating between illicit gaming information and other messages. Furthermore, it's much easier to encrypt messages, change addresses, and send and receive mail anonymously on the Internet.

And e-mail has no monolithic postal service. It relies on thousands of separate and wholly private service providers, many of which stridently object to enforcing a burdensome ban. Testifying before the National Gambling Impact Study Commission on behalf of over 250 ISPs, Ralph Simms said that the prohibitionists "imagine that problems of illegal content on the Internet could be resolved if ISPs assumed the role of traffic cop. This could not be further from the truth." Unless a gambling site rents space on an ISP's own server, Simms said, "the ISP has virtually no ability to control it."

Furthermore, American cops can do little to stop the explosion in legal gambling sites based in other countries. Such services can already set up shop in Australia, Antigua, Austria, Belgium, Costa Rica, the Dominican Republic, Finland, Germany, Grenada, Honduras, Liechtenstein, Mauritius, Vanuatu, and Venezuela, among other places. This growing number of overseas havens guarantees that, regardless of domestic policies, U.S. consumers will have access to Internet gambling.

Even Kyl admits that "we don't have jurisdiction over the people abroad who are doing it." To isolate Americans from the gaming traffic, he proposes to "pull the plug at the point of entry into the United States." But that traffic can enter the country from any number of overseas sites. To stop the trade, Kyl would have to "pull the plug" on every international Internet connection. He might as well demand a ban on horseless carriages.

Given those constraints, Kyl's bill cannot work as intended. It would, however, sorely compromise the cost, efficiency, and security of Internet communications; it would bring legal trouble to several otherwise innocent gamblers; and it would mock the rule of law.

Delayed Legalization

Fortunately, no full ban on Net gambling would likely survive, especially after cooler heads in the nation's revenue departments recognize the prohibited pastime as a new breed of cash cow. Prohibition, after all, merely ensures that bettors will ship their money to gambling sites based abroad; state governors and legislatures in the United States will soon demand a share of that bounty. The same political forces that have led to the widespread legalization of lottery, casino, and riverboat gaming will thus eventually embrace online gambling too. We can get there quickly and easily or slowly and painfully, but get there we almost certainly will.

By the same token, some in the existing gaming world do not fear competition from the Net as much as they want to take it on. The industry has thus taken the somewhat awkward position of demanding that Internet competitors share its regulatory burdens. "We cannot support it without tough regulation," American Gaming Association President Frank Fahrenkopf told the *Las Vegas Review-Journal* [in 1998].

Fahrenkopf and his allies prefer not to dwell on whether Internet gambling poses a competitive threat, nor do they publicly demand that it share their shackles simply to keep it from speeding ahead. They instead argue that the absence of regulation could lead to a scandal tainting the entire industry. It seems far more likely, however, that an Internet scandal would reaffirm the distinction between honorable old-timers and naughty onliners.

In all likelihood, the domestically licensed gambling industry simply wants to slow down its Internet competitors until it can join the race. Big-name casinos already sport some of the flashiest sites on the Web. Some, such as Caesar's Casino, run real sweepstakes online. The Hard Rock Casino has already set up space on its site for a virtual casino. Naturally, Kyl's bill includes an exemption for such online advertising and promotion. If and when U.S. lawmakers finally legalize Internet gambling, the incumbent industry will stand ready to cash in.

THE ADVANTAGES OF REGULATING INTERNET GAMBLING

Interactive Gaming Council

In September 2003 the National Conference of Legislators of Gaming States held meetings to discuss the status of legalized gambling. Among the organizations invited to comment was the Interactive Gaming Council (IGC), an international collective of trade associations involved with Internet gaming. In the following excerpt, from a paper submitted to this conference, the IGC argues that America's current ban on Internet gambling is doing more harm than good. According to the IGC, Americans already support Internet gambling by playing illegally, and many of these gamblers may end up victims of unscrupulous Web site owners because the online gaming industry is not subject to federal or state regulation. If, however, Internet gaming was legalized and regulated, then, the IGC claims, the industry could maintain Web site standards. The IGC also suggests that, as a viable industry, Internet gambling would profit state and federal governments by producing tax revenues. For these reasons, the IGC urges state legislators to help overturn the ban on Internet gaming and push for a regulated industry that will benefit all concerned. The IGC was originally formed in the United States in 1996, but given the government's current prohibitionist stance on Internet gaming, the organization relocated to Canada in 2000.

Gambling is currently one of the fastest growing forms of entertainment in the world. Internet gambling, however, has not been provided an opportunity for expansion, and in fact U.S. policy continues to restrict some of the world's most respected casino gaming companies from being competitive in this industry. This is in spite of statistics that show an estimated 1,800 gaming web sites with a projected gross income of $4.3 billion for 2003. . . .

MGM Mirage launched MGM Mirage Online in September 2001.

Interactive Gaming Council, letter to the National Conference of Legislators of Gaming States, December 3, 2003.

On June 30, 2003, the company announced it would cease operations of its Internet casino, playmgmmirage.com. In a statement released by the company, Terri Lanni, Chairman and CEO of MGM Mirage, indicated that MGM Mirage was able to prove Internet gaming can involve the same high standards as those expected from land-based casino licensees.

While MGM Mirage, through its online gaming web site operated from the Isle of Man since fall 2002, proved that a regulatory model for online gaming is workable, according to the company the closure of its operations resulted from an unclear, and potentially hostile political climate in the U.S. and other countries.

While the news was disappointing to advocates for licensure and regulation of online gaming, it was not surprising from a business perspective. In the press announcement, MGM Mirage indicated that it would take an approximate $5 million loss in discontinuing its Internet gaming operations. Clearly, you cannot run a business with opposition from U.S. policymakers when so much of the demand for Internet gaming is concentrated in North America. We think it is illogical for policymakers to continue toward a policy of prohibiting online gaming when such a policy only prevents the most responsible and experienced companies from entering the market. . . .

State governments will have to consider ways to protect the jobs and revenue currently created by the largest U.S. gaming companies when overseas competitors begin to provide online casino games to American residents. It is important to note that prohibiting the most respected gaming companies based in the U.S. as well as individual states themselves in terms of lotteries from participating in online gambling will not stop this competition. It makes more sense to develop a strict regulatory regime in the U.S. and let U.S. gaming companies lead the world and individual states preserve and protect revenues. While there will inevitably be some adjustments in the gaming world as offline and online companies learn to live with each other and deal with any dislocations in their respective industries, this is no different than Barnes and Noble learning to adjust to Amazon.com. . . .

The MGM Mirage decision to shut down its www.playmgmmirage .com web site is an example of how misguided public policy decisions are keeping the most responsible and reputable companies from entering this industry. A strictly regulated Internet gaming industry, which would include proper due diligence and continuous monitoring, would provide an opportunity for policymakers to protect citizens against underage and problem gambling as well as money laundering and at the same time produce additional revenues for governments and provide for job creation. The fear is that current policies are pushing the Internet gaming industry further underground, where there is less control, no revenue generation for states and no monies available to assist with player protection. . . .

Terri Lanni, Chairman and CEO of MGM Mirage, summarized the frustration of proponents of regulated Internet gaming in the U.S. in the MGM Mirage statement:

> Unfortunately, even in light of a successful working model, the legal and political climate in the U.S. and several other countries around the world remains unclear. The fact is that millions of U.S. citizens currently participate in online gaming in an unregulated environment. We believe that a more sound and realistic public policy would be to regulate the activity and hold operators to the highest standards of probity and integrity. . . .
>
> In the meantime, millions of U.S. citizens who are currently playing casino games online every day must continue to do so without the protections provided by common sense regulations that (we believe) should be implemented. . . .

Consumer Protection Concerns

In the opinion of the IGC [Interactive Gaming Council], much of the consumer protection issue should focus on protections for our most vulnerable citizens: children and problem gamblers. The issues of underage and problem gambling are crucial to the debate of online as well as any other form of gaming. After evaluating how to best protect the most vulnerable, the next step is to offer protections to those consumers that choose to play at online casino web sites.

In land-based gaming, jurisdictions devote significant resources to preventing minors from gambling. Obviously, the physical presence of minors helps to facilitate their identification. Yet, even with the opportunity presented by the physical presence of minors, no gaming jurisdiction is 100% effective in keeping minors from gambling, nor are jurisdictions 100% effective in controlling the purchase of tobacco and alcohol products by minors despite the person being physically present during the purchase. By contrast, many tools, including data cross checks, biometrics and geo-positioning and age verification software, are currently available to exclude minors and others from participating in gambling online. These technologies are rapidly improving in quality and are becoming increasingly cost-effective. Indeed, products such as iris and fingerprint recognition are being viewed as the next step forward for ATM card user verification. There are proposals in industry for a central registry where players who wish to be banned can register.

Unfortunately, there is no panacea for protecting youth. Rather, the IGC argues that the best strategy is a combination of social and educational interventions, technology-based tools and legal and regulatory approaches combined with parental control . . . NOT prohibition.

Similar arguments have been made with regard to problem gamblers. There appears to be an assumption that if pathological players must be present in a casino to gamble there is more of a chance that they can be identified and assisted. We have been unable to find any reliable data to back up this assumption. We believe that a computer-based system that allows a gambler to self-exclude or to establish loss limits stands a far greater chance of being effective than the systems in place in most casino jurisdictions today. In fact, computer technology provides an opportunity to identify patterns of behavior that may lead to problem gambling, and offer intervention when necessary. We concede that a gambler who is determined to gamble can hop from website to website, but a gambler who is determined to gamble can hop from one form of land-based gaming to another—including government-run lotteries with a prize pool in the millions of dollars and a return to player of not much over 50%. In the online world, rules of games and reports of a player's activities can be made readily available, as can contact details for bodies that aim to assist those with possible problem or compulsive gambling issues. . . .

The fact is that Internet gaming already exists. Billions of dollars are reportedly being bet over the Internet with little, if any, oversight or guarantee that the operators of these sites are fair and honest or that protections are in place to keep children and compulsive gamblers away. These revenue projections imply that a percentage of these monies are from American citizens and leave the U.S. with no subsequent benefit, directly or indirectly, to the U.S. or any individual state (including no dedicated funds for protecting children and problem gamblers through education or other programs). . . .

Taxation

This brings up the question of taxation. How can states tax online gaming operators? Taxation is a complex (and controversial) area of e-commerce, but as policy makers are beginning to understand, the taxation issue is important and not impossible. In our experience, state governments would have several options available with regard to taxation, with no serious debate on this topic occurring to date. Whichever method a state regulatory jurisdiction decides with regard to taxation, the bottom line is additional revenue to that jurisdiction.

State legislators should consider at least two issues with regard to taxation. One is tax generation within an individual state, where players would only be allowed to participate from within a single state's jurisdiction (and perhaps also accept players from overseas). The other is tax sharing among states that move toward a cooperative regulatory framework for online gaming.

In either case, legislators and policymakers could decide to tax online gaming operators on gross income or require operators to identify gross win from each participating state, with a tax distribution made to each individual state based on the residence of player participation. In addition, a strictly regulated environment would allow the best opportunity for state governments to collect tax based on player winnings. It is not intended that any cooperation between states would allow for infringement on another state's rights if that state chooses not to license and regulate online gaming. . . .

Online Regulation

If individual states looked toward regulation, rather than prohibition of online gaming, how would Internet Gambling Regulation Work? Internet gaming regulation must be based on the same principals as the regulations established for traditional, brick and mortar casinos. Put simply, regulators must have the power to ensure honesty, integrity and the financial security of operators and to oversee the integrity of the games being offered.

In any traditional gaming jurisdiction, a person or company cannot receive a license to operate a casino unless they undergo an intensive background investigation, and the casino regulators find them to possess the highest degree of good character, honesty and integrity. Regulators could perform the same kind of investigation and qualification of Internet gaming operators in exactly the same way it is done for traditional gaming. The proof is evident in the regulations already established in several countries throughout the world. Internet gaming regulations may not be perfect at the beginning, but just as with traditional gaming regulations, a more efficient regulatory scheme will evolve over time. . . .

Suitability investigations will be paramount to ensure the character, honesty and integrity of the licensees. A cursory suitability investigation will not be acceptable. Those applying for licenses in land-based casinos are subject to extensive background investigations and the same should be true for Internet gaming operators.

Just like regulation of traditional casinos, there cannot be any short cuts with regard to suitability, especially in the infancy of Internet gaming. Any regulatory structure would have to be particularly sensitive of all the allegations and rumors of impropriety over the Internet. The suspicion and mistrust of Internet gambling that exists must be countered by strict regulations allowing only those with impeccable suitability to be licensed, the same requirements as established for traditional casino licensing. There should be no difference in the licensing process between a traditional gaming license and an Internet gaming license. . . .

The regulating body must be able to ensure the consumer that Internet gaming operators are legitimate, that operators offer fair and honest games and that they have the financial stability to pay winnings to its players. . . .

Casino regulators should check and monitor all gaming equipment and the conduct of the games themselves to make sure the games are honest and offer patrons a fair chance of winning. . . . If we can test the computer chips and gaming software in [land-based] gaming jurisdictions throughout the world, there is no reason we could not inspect and verify the software used for Internet gaming. Operators and government need to create systems that, at the most basic level, allow a gambler to know that their $10 wager will provide them with the same opportunity of winning as if they were to wager the same $10 at a traditional casino.

It Makes More Sense to Legalize and Regulate

Internet gaming is a complex policy issue for governments and regulators in every corner of the world. The simple solution is to make Internet gaming illegal, and hope to forget about it.

The acceptance of a global market for online gaming is a reality unless the Internet itself is banned, something that is unlikely. It is important to recognize that prohibiting U.S. gaming companies as well as individual states themselves, whether it be operating an online casino or operating online lotteries, from participating in online gambling will not stop Internet competition. It makes more sense to develop a strict regulatory regime and let U.S. companies lead the world and allow individual states to protect and increase revenues.

CHAPTER 4

THE SOCIAL
CONSEQUENCES OF
LEGALIZED GAMBLING

THE REVENUE FROM STATE-RUN LOTTERIES BENEFITS THE STATES

Blake Hart and Jonathan Sofley

In the following article Blake Hart and Jonathan Sofley argue that lotteries are an effective way to finance public services. Lotteries have flourished in America since their inception, Hart and Sofley maintain, because they are a voluntary method of raising revenues—an alternative to undesirable tax increases. The authors also assert that lottery proceeds can fund education programs and scholarships, both of which are tangible benefits that have wide public appeal. Given these and other advantages, Hart and Sofley conclude, states can ill afford to dispense with lotteries. Hart and Sofley are public affairs graduate students at Western Carolina University in North Carolina.

The current economic climate in the United States has adversely affected almost every corner of the marketplace. With most sectors of the work force experiencing layoffs and hiring freezes, less money is coming into households, and, as a consequence, states and local communities are receiving less revenue from tax collection. States are continuously in search of revenue to supplement rapidly declining general funds. This search has drawn many state legislatures to support state-sanctioned lotteries as a viable measure to increase state revenues.

Economic decline has spurred state governments to find ways to meet financial needs without imposing new or higher taxes on local residents. State lotteries provide a valid means of voluntary taxation to allow for such worthy goals as the growth of education, welfare programs, and transportation upgrades. Without a state lottery, legislators are compelled to impose higher taxes upon citizens to meet these needs. Lotteries thus provide essential funds for state programs through voluntary taxation.

Lottery History

Lotteries have been a tool used by governments, civic groups, and private charities to fund public services for over 500 years. The first com-

Blake Hart and Jonathan Sofley, "State Lotteries Are Needed," *International Social Science Review*, Spring/Summer 2004. Copyright © 2004 by Phi Gamma Mu. Reproduced by permission.

mercial lotteries appeared in Belgium in the 1400s, gained popularity, and spread across Europe to Italy and England. American history provides several examples of lotteries used to benefit states and their citizens. In 1826, for example, the Virginia legislature granted former President Thomas Jefferson authorization to hold a lottery to sell his properties in order to alleviate some of the large debts he had accumulated. Jefferson, however, never actually held his lottery. In seeking to rebuild the South after the Civil War, Southern states used lotteries to fund state programs. Currently, a number of states use the lottery to fund public services. Georgia, South Carolina, and Tennessee each use state lotteries to support education programs. The state lottery is an attractive option to legislators because citizens are not compelled to contribute and state revenue is enhanced by the proceeds of this "voluntary form of taxation," [as researchers Donald E. Miller and Patrick A. Pierce state].

In his essay "Financing Public Goods by Means of Lotteries," the economist John Morgan argues that "relative to the standard voluntary contributions mechanism, lotteries: (a) increase the provision of the public good; (b) are welfare improving; and, (c) provide levels of public good close to first-best as the size of the lottery prize increases." In short, lotteries benefit states. Proceeds from state lotteries go towards public goods such as education, or, in the case of Indiana, transportation. Not only do funds collected through state lotteries help primary and secondary education, they also contribute to the welfare of individuals as educational lotteries allow those who could not afford higher education to receive financial assistance for a college education. Since state lotteries support the public interest by contributing to public services, they are a useful and viable financial resource for states.

Lottery Benefits

Properly managed state-sanctioned lottery programs have helped states raise over thirty billion dollars in revenue nationally. Many states reserve lottery proceeds for certain areas such as university scholarship funds and early childhood programs. This system has been especially successful in Georgia, which, in 1995, "provided $85 million in scholarships which allowed more than 100,000 Georgia high school graduates to receive post secondary education . . . also $157 million allowed 48,000 four year olds to attend free pre-kindergarten," [write P. Edward French and Ronald E. Stanley].

Another public benefit derived from state lotteries is found in the jobs created by these lotteries and the programs they help fund. More than 8,000 jobs in Georgia are directly attributable to the state lottery and its funded programs. These newly created jobs have produced $342 million in personal income in the state. As a consequence, the lottery is now the fourth largest source of revenue in Georgia, trailing only personal income tax, general sales tax, and corporate income tax.

The success of Georgia and other state lotteries can be traced, in part, to the large influx of money from neighboring states that lack such games of chance. North Carolinians, with no state lottery of their own, spend $100 million dollars annually participating in Virginia's lottery. South Carolinians have sent $95 million dollars a year in lottery monies to subsidize Georgia's state education system. Large amounts of money leaving a state's borders hurt the economy and exacerbate state budget problems. This is causing more states to debate the pros and cons of implementing a lottery.

States can also profit from lotteries because of the economic benefits of providing relief to state taxpayers. The Wisconsin state legislature, for example, has given its citizens close to two billion dollars in property tax relief since that state's lottery began in 1988. Such benefits are not uncommon. It is thus evident that the state lottery is an effective means to raise needed funds voluntarily without raising taxes. When effective administration of this money is achieved, the public can benefit from this windfall of revenue.

Public Choice and Public Good

Adults who value the chance to win big in the lottery more than they value the money they are spending to do so will participate in such games of chance. These adults make independent decisions concerning how they will spend their limited resources. No distinction can be made between lottery advertising and the alluring propaganda of fast food restaurants or alcoholic beverages, both of which have incredibly adverse effects on those who routinely consume those products, and from which the state receives considerable tax revenues. The risks and failures of state lotteries are as well documented as their benefits and successes. Adults have to be the lone stewards over their individual finances however they choose to allocate them. When effective administration of lottery revenue is achieved, the proceeds can accomplish a great deal of good.

State Lottery Benefits to Education Are Exaggerated

Marjorie Coeyman

According to Marjorie Coeyman, a staff writer for the *Christian Science Monitor*, the fact that lottery proceeds are earmarked for education is what makes state-run lotteries acceptable to the public. In the following article Coeyman reports, however, that not all lottery earnings go toward education. As lottery profits increase, a larger percentage of the money may be siphoned off to pay taxes, Coeyman notes, and some states even direct their lottery proceeds to cover lottery advertising costs and to build up larger jackpots. Higher lottery returns may therefore translate into a very small net increase in the funds allocated to education, Coeyman states.

The selling point for state lotteries was that they would steer money to education. The actual results are a bit more mixed.

[In 2003], millions of dollars of Indiana state lottery proceeds were poured into a teachers' retirement fund, school technology, and public-school tuition support.

[In 2004], the Idaho state lottery contributed $9 million to build new roofs on schoolhouses, new bleachers in school stadiums, and to buy new computers and school buses. Two years ago in California the state lottery contributed a record $1.11 billion to public education.

All this sounds good. But the story behind lottery money for education is more complicated, and not as rosy.

"The proceeds from state lotteries are less than you might think," says Molly Burke, researcher at the Education Commission of the States in Denver. "Even if they're all earmarked toward education, it isn't a huge amount. It's never quite as much as states would like the schools and the taxpayers to think."

Where the Money Goes

Since the 1970s and 1980s, state lotteries have been popular means of helping to fill state coffers. [As of July 2003] 39 states have lotteries

Marjorie Coeyman, "Lottery Isn't Always a Boon to Schools," *Christian Science Monitor*, vol. 95, July 15, 2003, pp. 14, OP, 1C. Copyright © 2003 by The Christian Science Publishing Society. All rights reserved. Reproduced by permission from *Christian Science Monitor*, www.csmonitor.com.

and several more have voted to join the crowd. Many states sell the lottery concept to the public with the promise that a large portion of the proceeds will benefit public schools.

In fact, 22 states earmark portions of lottery earnings for public school spending. States such as New York, Michigan, Missouri, and Vermont plow 100 percent of their lottery gains back into public education.

Not Always a Gain for Schools

Yet, while the public may believe that means a net gain for schools, that's not always the case.

Many times, says the Rev. Richard McGowan, a professor at the Carroll School of Management at Boston College, "you're really allowing the state to spend the money in other places rather than the schools. It's not a bonus for the schools but a substitution."

Sometimes what ends up happening is that schools achieve a small gain through the lottery.

"The fact that you vote for a lottery that's going to add $100 million to education doesn't mean that education will get $100 million," says John Augenblick, president of Augenblick, Paliach & Associates, a consulting firm in Denver that specializes in state education-policy finances.

"The government may take back $75 million in property taxes. There's probably a net gain, but it's not large."

Yet in Ohio, pouring lottery proceeds into education actually caused state spending on schools to shrink, according to a study by graduate student Thomas Garnett published by the Buckeye Institute in Dayton, Ohio.

The study demonstrated that, after Ohio's 1974 promise to devote all lottery winnings to public schools, state spending on education dropped from 42 percent of its total budget in 1973 to 29 percent in 1994.

A Question of Management

Of course, not all lotteries are equal. Many policymakers praise Georgia's state lottery, which funnels all its proceeds into specific projects related to education.

Instead of pouring money into a general fund, the law in Georgia restricts lottery profits to financing college scholarships, universal prekindergarten, and technology grants for schools.

There is also a danger in such a system, however. Because some of these projects are funded solely through the lottery, if lottery proceeds ever dry up, important programs could find themselves high and dry.

But overall, if all state lotteries were designed like the Georgia model, says Father McGowan, education might receive a genuine benefit.

More states are leaning that way. Texas has already adopted a similar plan, while Tennessee, North Carolina, and South Carolina have
all approved lotteries based on the Georgia model.

All these states plan to donate their full proceeds to educational
programs.

But the overall financial success of state lotteries is uneven as well.
Massachusetts, which permits no advertising for its lottery and de-
votes all its profits to spending on local schools and cities, is sometimes called the most efficient of all state lotteries.

California, on the other hand, is sometimes criticized as an ineffi-
cient lottery hampered by poorly conceived restrictions.

Some states spend so heavily on lottery prizes and related advertising that their proceeds are thin and may vary dramatically from year
to year.

Of course, even when lotteries are not most profitably managed,
there are certain residual benefits to linking state lotteries to spending
for schools, says Mr. Augenblick.

One is that politicians sell lotteries to the public by stressing the
paramount need to fund public education. If nothing else, Augenblick
says, their campaigning serves to reenforce the message that spending
on school is both important and taken seriously.

"They get the issue in front of people that there ought to be more
money for education," he says. "And then the support of the people
tells politicians that this does matter to voters."

No Major Gains from an Age-Old Institution

There are also those who argue that, however marginal the financial
contribution of the lotteries may be, those few extra dollars may make
a difference.

Last year in Illinois, where all lottery proceeds go to education, lottery earnings accounted for 3 percent of the total $18.61 billion the
state spent on education.

"If you believe that 1 percent is critical—and some people do," says
Augenblick, "then all of these lotteries are important. But you're not
talking about the bulk of anything."

The idea of raising money for schools through lotteries has been an
American tradition since Colonial times, McGowan says.

Both Harvard and Columbia Universities, he points out, helped finance some of their earliest buildings through lotteries.

"It was a tradition," McGowan says.

But today, he adds, state lotteries have become a type of institution. "I don't think they can be cut now," he says. "Once it gets in
there, the state becomes pretty dependent on this for revenue."

What's likely for the future is more state involvement in lotteries
and other forms of gambling as well, McGowan forecasts.

Games of chance will continue to be frequently pegged to education because it's an effective way to overcome public qualms about legal gambling.

That's not necessarily a bad thing for school financing, says Augenblick—but neither is it a tremendously good thing.

"The state lotteries are good," he says. "They're better than nothing. But the're not nearly as good as they're sold to people to be."

STATE LOTTERIES PREY ON THE POOR

Evangelical Lutheran Church in America

The Lutheran Church views gambling as a human weakness that often leads to problems for society and especially for the family unit. For this reason, on its Web site the Evangelical Lutheran Church in America posts a collection of arguments against gambling. One of these documents, reprinted here, specifically warns of how state-sanctioned lotteries prey on the poorest members of society. The church argues that lottery advertising attempts to convince people that winning a jackpot is a way to lift oneself out of poverty. Indeed, according to the Lutheran Church, studies have proven that the largest percentage of lottery income comes from those who can least afford to play. Particularly troubling to the church, though, is that for some of these players, the promise of winning big becomes an addiction that quickly brings already-impoverished lives to ruin.

The modern experience of state-run lotteries in this country begins with New Hampshire in 1964. In a story that would be repeated across the country, New Hampshire faced a difficult choice: either raise taxes or institute a lottery. To politicians and citizens alike, the choice was, and has continued to be, an easy one. In 1996, states earned well over $10 billion from lotteries. Where tax increases generate predictable hostility, the lottery offers a "voluntary tax"; revenue pours into public treasuries from the pockets of willing participants. With this combination of increased revenues without new taxes, few should be surprised that lotteries have spread to all but a handful of states. But easy choices, as we all know, are not necessarily the right choices. St. Paul's admonition that we not use our liberty at the expense of the vulnerable is especially appropriate here.

The Poor Fund the Lotteries

Our foremost concern with lotteries is their impact on the poor. As studies have shown—including those conducted by lotteries themselves—poor people spend a much larger proportion of their income

The Evangelical Lutheran Church in America, "Division for Church in Society: Session 4: Lotteries, the Poor, and the State," www.elca.org, December 3, 2004. Reproduced by permission.

on the lottery than do those in middle- or upper-income brackets. In fact, recent studies suggest that the poor spend more on the lottery in *absolute*, not merely proportional, terms. If we conduct state lotteries principally because they raise public funds, then lotteries seem to violate our strong commitment to progressive taxation—the idea that those who are better able to pay should bear a greater portion of public burdens. At the very least, the costs of our common projects should not fall disproportionately on the poor.

The lotteries' defenders respond that this charge of "regressive taxation" implies that the poor are coerced, when no one is forced to play. While true, the defense underestimates the significance of lottery advertising, which tends to undercut the stress on voluntariness. The state does not merely tolerate lottery expenditures, as it does with other "sin tax" items like alcohol and cigarettes; the state actively encourages people to play. Unless state law requires the lottery to disclose the true odds of winning (and few do), lottery ads generally overstate or obscure the chances of winning, in order to make the worst bet in gambling seem attractive. Black jack tables return 98% of the wagered money back to winners, and casino slot machines return 92%, but lotteries generally pay out around 50% of the amount wagered. And the odds of winning a large jackpot are astronomical (up to 1 in 80 million for certain multi-state lotteries). A person who buys a ticket in that lottery is forty times more likely to be hit by lightning than to win the jackpot.

Targeting the Poor

Beyond misrepresented odds, lottery advertisers target the poor in ways that are particularly troubling. Lottery ads prey on a sense of economic hopelessness, claiming to offer a real chance of financial success—a chance that work and saving, the messages seems to suggest, cannot provide. Ads promise to take you from "your street to easy street," or show pictures of people who go from tattered clothes one moment to tuxedos, champagne and expensive cars, proclaiming "It could happen to you!" The lotteries' claim that "there is nothing wrong with dreaming" becomes even more suspect in light of their advertising strategies. Billboards and radio commercials focus on lower-income areas and markets, while ad campaigns and new games are timed to coincide with the release of government benefit checks. Lotteries are sold the same way as any other product: identify likely consumers, then stimulate their desire.

Of course, the lottery isn't just another product, and the state isn't just another business. First, to say the least, it is something of an anomaly that the state, which we believe to be God's instrument for achieving the temporal common good, now promotes greed and denigrates work and saving. As social commentators William Galston and David Wasserman write, "The state's promotion of gambling belies its commitment to reducing the influence of morally arbitrary factors on the lives of its citizens and to supporting the virtues of thrift, hard work, and responsibility." Second, the deceptive nature of lottery advertising contributes to a general and corrosive distrust for the word of government officials. Third, by raising revenues through lotteries—the "easy way"—public officials bypass an important step in political accountability: decisions about taxation provide an occasion for debating the proper functions and objects of government. Where something needs be done for the common good, the community should fund it; but if the community is unwilling to support a particular project, then we should seriously question the state's justification in pursuing it. And fourth, the lottery represents a betrayal of the state's special responsibility for the vulnerable. Through deception and by preying on their desperation, the state takes from the poor what they can little afford to give.

States Are Dependent on Lotteries

Despite these concerns, there seems little chance for returning to an era when states did not promote gambling. As we have seen over the last few years, compulsive gamblers are not the only ones who are addicted: given the general anti-tax atmosphere, state officials have come to depend on lottery revenues in their budgeting. The problem is that lottery revenues are not always dependable, especially as additional forms of gambling come on the scene. When lottery revenues start to decline, officials look to more exciting games: in the 1970s this meant weekly and then daily drawings, and finally instant games. In the late 1980s and through the 1990s, even those games began to fail to hold players' attention, so lotteries have turned to even faster games like keno and video lottery. And the faster games do generate revenues: South Dakota's video lottery terminals account for a significant majority of the state lottery's revenues, and a 1996 Oregon study noted that video poker revenues in a two-year period were more than the total state lottery revenues from the six years before the video games were introduced. The increased revenue may be a blessing to the state treasury, but it seems to have been a curse to pathological gamblers. At more than ten games a minute, gamblers liken the machines to "crack" cocaine—quick to addict and quick to bring the addict to ruin. That states would rush to supply these machines, especially under the deceptive cloak of a "lottery," gives further evidence of the problems noted above.

CASINO GAMBLING CAUSES CRIME

Earl L. Grinols

In the following article Earl L. Grinols argues that many casino communities witness increases in crime. According to Grinols, while crime may not rise immediately after the opening of a casino, within five years of casino operation, statistics typically reveal increases in robbery, assault, rape, auto theft, and other crimes in the surrounding community. Part of the explanation for this increase, Grinols notes, is the growing number of problem gamblers that frequent casinos. The most troubled of these compulsive players often turn to theft, burglary, and other criminal acts to pay off the huge debts they amass as a result of their gambling disorder, Grinols claims. Earl L. Grinols is a professor of economics at the University of Illinois in Urbana. He has written many articles on government monetary policy and is the author of *Gambling in America: Costs and Benefits*.

Evidence is converging to show that casino gambling causes significant increases in crime. Taken altogether, casinos impose crime and other costs—paid for by society, including those who do not gamble—that exceed their benefits and represent substantial burdens on nearby populations. Because casino gambling fails a cost-benefit test, policymakers should give serious consideration to options that include imposing taxes equal to the costs casinos impose, restricting casino expansion, or banning casino gambling altogether.

Crime is affected by multiple factors including population density, the number of males and females in different age ranges, percent of each age group that is white, percent of each age group that is black, per capita personal income, unemployment rates, per capita retirement compensation, per capita income maintenance payments, and "shall issue" laws (giving citizens the right to carry concealed firearms upon request—believed to reduce certain crimes). Hence, connecting any single cause such as casinos to crime is controversial. Only by careful sifting of a large body of data can the effect of casinos be separated from other causes to establish a connection. The gambling in-

Earl L. Grinols, "Casino Gambling Causes Crime," *Policy Forum*, vol. 13, November 2, 2000. Copyright © 2000 by the University of Illinois, Institute of Government and Public Affairs. Reproduced by permission.

dustry naturally has resisted research findings that link casinos to more crime.

How do researchers conclude that casinos cause crime and measure the size of the connection? There are two ways—the first is through the study of problem and pathological gamblers and the second is through statistical analysis of crime numbers.

Problem Gambling Leads to Crime

Pathological gambling is a recognized impulse control disorder of the Diagnostic and Statistical Manual (DSM-IV) of the American Psychiatric Association. Pathological gamblers (often referred to as "addicted" or "compulsive" gamblers) are identified by a number of characteristics including repeated failures to resist the urge to gamble, loss of control over their gambling, personal lives and employment, reliance on others to relieve a desperate financial situation caused by gambling, and the committing of illegal acts to finance gambling. Problem gamblers have similar problems, but to a lesser degree.

It appears that a significant proportion of the population is susceptible to problem or pathological gambling. The latent propensity becomes overt when the opportunity to gamble is provided and sufficient time has elapsed for the problem to manifest. Pathological gamblers are generally found to constitute one or two percent of the population and problem gamblers are another two to three percent in areas where casino gambling is available. One study of gamblers in treatment found that 62 percent committed illegal acts as a result of their gambling. Eighty percent had committed civil offenses and 23 percent were charged with criminal offenses, according to a 1990 Maryland Department of Health and Mental Hygiene survey. A similar survey of nearly 400 members of Gambler's Anonymous showed that 57 percent admitted stealing to finance their gambling. Moreover, the amounts are not small. On average they stole $135,000, and total theft was over $30 million, according to the testimony of Henry Lesieur from the Institute of Problem Gambling before the National Gambling Impact Study Commission, Atlantic City, New Jersey, January 22, 1998. The National Gambling Impact Study Commission's final report issued in June 1999 reported that among those who did not gamble (had not gambled in the past year) only 7 percent had ever been incarcerated. In contrast, more than three times this number (21.4 percent) of individuals who had been pathological gamblers at any point during their lifetime had been incarcerated.

By tallying up the crimes of pathological and problem gamblers and the associated costs to society such as police, apprehension, adjudication, and incarceration costs, the average crime costs to society of an additional pathological or problem gambler (some studies lump the two groups together) can be determined. Recent research using this methodology found that an average problem gambler costs society $10,112 per year. Crime costs constituted $4,225, or 42 percent of these costs.

Combining crime costs with studies of the prevalence of pathological and problem gamblers provides crime cost figures for society as a whole. Using the numbers just reported implies annual crime costs per adult capita of $57. This number can be compared to the crime costs found by the second method for relating casinos to crime.

Looking at Crime Rates

A second way to determine the effect of casinos on crime is to look directly at aggregate crime statistics. The advantage is that the method is direct, and—because it looks at more than just the crimes committed by problem and pathological gamblers—it is more inclusive. The disadvantage is that it may be difficult to distinguish the share of crime related to casinos from the mass of other crime that occurs all the time. Moreover, the period of major casino expansion in the United States, 1991 to 1997, coincides with a period of secular *decline* in overall crime rates. It would be tempting, therefore, to observe that crime fell after a particular casino was introduced and from this conclude that the casino reduced crime. Such a conclusion would be false if crime would have fallen even further without the casino. Finally, because the effects of casinos might differ in different areas, a large sample could be needed to reliably pinpoint the truth.

In research conducted at the University of Illinois and the University of Georgia and with these factors in mind, Professor David Mustard, Cynthia Hunt Dilley and I examined crime statistics for all 3,165 counties in the United States for twenty years beginning with year 1977. This period covers the period of introduction of casinos in all counties with the exception of Nevada. The number of offenses for the 7 FBI Index I offenses (robbery, aggravated assault, rape, murder, larceny, burglary, and auto theft) was obtained from the Federal Bureau of Investigation's Uniform Crime Report County-Level Data. We obtained U.S. Census Bureau data to control for demographic, income, and other variables that affect crime as described above. In all, 54 variables were used to explain observed crime rates across counties and time. We included twelve variables to identify each year from four years before the opening of the first casino in a county to seven years after it opened. These variables serve two purposes: first, to distinguish the effects of casinos from changes that preceded their opening (for example, a trend toward lawlessness conceivably could lead to the opening of a casino instead of the reverse); and second, to sort out the timing of those effects (an effect on crime could take several years to develop). To find the dates for the first casino opening we contacted state gaming authorities in every state, called casinos to find opening date or date of first Class III gambling (in many cases casinos began as bingo halls and switched at a later date), and used casino in-

ternet website information to check our data. The final list was veri-
fied against the annually produced *Executive's Guide to North American
Casinos*.

Deciphering the Data

What did the data show? If property crime rates are indexed so that
1982 rates equal 100, then the crime rate in 1991 was 99.7 in non-
casino counties (counties that had no casinos during the sample period) and 100.3 in casino counties (counties that had a casino by the
end of the sample period)—hardly any difference at all. However,
looking at the same statistic just 5 years later—after casinos had begun operation in the majority of the casino counties—the indexes
stood at 82.1 for non-casino counties and 93.7 for casino counties.
The raw data suggests, therefore, that 12.4 percent of the crime observed in casino counties would not be there if casinos were absent. A
similar picture emerges for violent crimes.

The problem with using the raw data for inferences, however, is
that direct comparisons do not take into account other factors that
cause crime. For example, it is well known that crime rates in areas of
high population density tend to be higher. What if between 1991 and
1996 casino counties experienced a significant increase in their population density? Then some or all of the increased crime might be due
to the change in population density. This is why we collected so
many other variables and applied regression procedures to them—to
separate the changes in crime rates due to other factors from those
due to casinos.

After adjusting for all of the other factors an interesting picture begins to emerge, both in terms of the share of crime in casino counties
due to casinos and in terms of the pattern that the changes take over
time. The data indicated that compared to non-casino counties there
was no discernable difference in crime in casino counties in the four
years before casinos opened that could be attributed to the opening of
casinos. (We did not expect to find any connection, so this finding
was anticipated.) For the first three years after the casino began operation, there also was no significant impact on crime rates. After the
third year, however, crime rates began to rise in casino counties compared to those without casinos. By 1996, casinos accounted for 10.3
percent of the observed violent crime and 7.7 percent of the observed
property crime in casino counties. Estimates of the share of crime attributable to casinos in 1996 for individual crimes ranged from 3 to
30 percent. Auto theft was the highest, followed by robbery at 20 percent. (In addition to stealing an auto, auto theft includes taking parts
of cars such as expensive sound equipment as well as things from or
out of a car.) The values for the rest of the offenses were between 3
and 10 percent.

Criminologists in the late 1980s and early 1990s estimated the cost per victimization of different types of crime. Applying these costs to the implied number of offenses for each crime due to casinos and dividing by the adult population of casino counties in 1996 produced an annual cost for casino-induced crime of $63 per adult capita. This figure is remarkably close to the $57 per adult capital crime cost estimated through the study of problem and pathological gamblers.

CASINO GAMBLING DOES NOT CAUSE CRIME

David Waddell

David Waddell is a Michigan lawyer who teaches at the Thomas M. Cooley Law School. He is also the coauthor of *The State of Michigan Gaming Law Legal Resource Book* and publishes the *Michigan Gaming Law Newsletter*. In the following selection Waddell states that before the state of Michigan decided to legalize casino gambling, antigambling forces warned that a host of social ills—including an increase in crime—would follow. Waddell reports, however, that the predicted crime wave never materialized. As Waddell asserts, statistics did show a rise in crime, but the rise was not dramatic nor was it inconsistent with the rise in crime rates that commonly accompanies the opening of any tourist attraction. Studies in other cities also found no direct correlation between the presence of casinos and acute rises in crime, Waddell notes. Most telling, he argues, is that the crime rates in Detroit actually dropped three years after the city's casinos opened, disproving the claims of casino opponents.

Before the casino referendum passed in Michigan, there were the usual dire predictions of the impact of casinos on crime in the City of Detroit. Would the overall rate of crime go up, or would the increased employment and boost to the economy the casinos would bring result in a lower crime rate. As discussed below, preliminary statistics suggest that crime has actually declined in the City of Detroit since the introduction of casinos. Yet, based on the reports in the mainstream media, one would think that the casinos have had the opposite effect.

Grant Stitt, Chairman of the University of Nevada-Reno Department of Criminal Justice, told *The Las Vegas Sun* that residents of communities introducing casino gaming often perceived that crime went up more than it actually did. Mr. Stitt stated, "That (the perception of crime) in itself is a significant factor, because you have to deal with communities based on what people think. They may not go to places they used to because they're concerned about being victimized. We don't understand why people think that."

He further stated, "Anytime you build a tourist attraction, you increase crime. You have an influx of tourists that are ready victims. They're relaxing and not on guard about being victimized." Mr. Stitt continued, "You could open a Six Flags (amusement park) in Sheboygan, Wisconsin, and the crime rate in Sheboygan could go up because you have numbers of tourists coming into your community." Mr. Stitt's comments fall directly in line with the reality of crime rates. If more people are introduced to a particular area, the number of individual incidents will likely go up regardless as to whether you open a zoo, a theme park or a casino. Yet, as a percentage of the population circulating in a community, the actual amount of crime can be significantly lower.

Studies Show No Consistency

A study conducted by the University of Nevada-Reno Institute for the Study of Gambling and Commercial Gaming supports the idea that casino gambling is simply another form of entertainment and that those who participate represent the general population. The study is entitled, "The Effect of Casino Gambling on Crime in New Casino Jurisdictions," and tracks the effect of casinos on crime in seven different cities that had recently introduced casino gambling. The cities were Biloxi, MS; St. Louis City, St. Louis County and St. Joseph, MO; Alton and Peoria, IL; and Sioux City, IA. The report states that,

"The seven jurisdictions each initiated casino gambling in the 1990's and have had casino gambling for a minimum of four years. This time frame allows comparisons to be made before and after casinos were in operation. Comparing the before and after crime rates, the data revealed few consistent trends in crime. In three communities, there were many more crimes that significantly increased than decreased. In three other jurisdictions, there were many more crimes that significantly decreased than increased. In one city, the vast majority of crimes showed no change. Few statistically significant changes are found in pre and post casino periods. It is plausible that the effects of casinos in a community are quite varied, depending on a multitude of variables."

These results illustrate the fact that casino gambling may have no significant effect on crime rates per se and notes that any increase or decrease in crime rates depends on the human element, and cannot be predicted. Crime rates rise and fall periodically in all cities and locations regardless of whether they have a casino or not. One could potentially make the argument that bringing casinos into a particular location could decrease the occurrence of specific crimes just as easily as one can argue that the introduction of casino gambling raises crime rates.

Decreasing Crime Rate in Detroit

Each day, more than 50,000 gamblers walk into one of the three Detroit casinos. Out of this huge group of people it is inevitable that there will be some small number of people who do bad things at some point in their lives. When caught, it is not surprising that they are quick to make excuses to try to elicit sympathy. The popular misconceptions and myths about the casino gambling industry provide a ready target for this type of excuse making. Unfortunately, the media is all too often a willing accomplice in further promulgating such myths. After all, a headline that reads "Casino Losers Rob Banks" probably makes "good copy" and sells papers, even if it fails to see the forest through the trees.

According to Detroit's Official Uniform Crime Report, provided by the Detroit Police Department's Crime Analysis Unit, Part I crimes (including homicide, rape, robbery, assault, burglary and larceny) have dropped drastically by an impressive 24% since casino gaming was introduced to the city. In 1998, prior to casino gaming in Detroit, 117,911 Part I crimes were committed. In 2001, after three years of casino gaming in Detroit, 90,193 Part I crimes were committed. That is nearly 30,000 fewer Part I crimes committed in Detroit since casino gaming debuted in the city. Since 1998, the year before casinos came to Detroit, homicide is down 8%, assault is down 12%, robbery is down 17%, burglary is down a whopping 30% and larceny is down an amazing 32%. The crime rate in Detroit has decreased in every major category since casinos were introduced to the city. . . . These statistics offer simple proof that introducing casino gaming into a community does not increase crime.

What is astounding to me is the lack of outrage expressed by members of the casino industry and casino patrons to such misguided attacks. I can think of no other industry that is subjected to such continuous unsubstantiated abuse. Too often, opponents of casino gambling quote single lines of scientific studies out of context to support their theories while ignoring the overall conclusions reached as a result of the study. Some of the broad over-generalizations that result are, quite simply, offensive. There are many good people who enjoy their visits to the casino without becoming the evil monsters that the media portrays them as potentially becoming.

Personal Responsibility

Left out of all of these attacks is one very simple, common sense concept called PERSONAL RESPONSIBILITY. People who are hell-bent on self destruction will find some means of doing it, whether it be alcohol, drugs, food addiction, smoking or problem gambling. In most cases, these individuals use more than one method to self destruct.

What the casinos have brought to such individuals is a real opportunity for treatment through substantial funding of counseling programs for such addicts. This is funding that prior to the introduction of casinos in Detroit did not exist despite a significant number of problem gamblers who were either betting illegally on the Internet, or who were going to Canada, charity nights, the tracks, the state lottery, tribal casinos, bingo, the "friendly neighborhood poker games," office pools or betting on their golf matches.

Personal responsibility means getting help when it is needed. The Detroit casinos, through millions of dollars of contributions, have assured that the help is there. The casinos in Detroit promote the availability of counseling through the funding of signs within their properties; bill boards on Michigan freeways; T.V. or radio commercials; and newspaper ads that you see all across Michigan. That may not make good page one copy or sell many papers, but it is the truth.

COMPULSIVE GAMBLING IS A GROWING PROBLEM

Dan Horn

Dan Horn is a reporter for the *Cincinnati Enquirer*. In the following article he cites evidence from his home city and the nation at large that suggests problem gambling is on the rise. According to Horn, problem gambling—a pathological disorder that prompts many gamblers to wager beyond their limits and follow such losses with even more gambling—affects millions of Americans. The disorder can have grave consequences for players, including bankruptcy, poor job performance, and strained relationships with family and friends, Horn reports. While many interested organizations—including the gaming industry—are helping to establish treatment programs for compulsive gamblers, there is still no solution to the growing problem, Horn concludes.

From the moment he woke up each morning, Fred's day was all about gambling.

First the 58-year-old from Northern Kentucky checked the late sports scores on TV and added up his wins and losses. Then he called his bookie with bets for that night's games.

By late morning, he'd head out to the track to bet the horses, or to a poker game with some friends. If it was a weekend, he might drive to the casinos in Atlantic City.

By nightfall he was back in front of a TV, watching the games he'd bet on.

When he finally quit gambling 14 years ago, Fred had lost his house, his business and more than $100,000. He'd even considered suicide, figuring it was the only way to be sure he'd never gamble again.

"It was all day, seven days a week," says Fred, who asked that his full name not be used. "The gambling was more important to me than anything."

Millions Take the Risk

As [former baseball player and team manager] Pete Rose makes headlines and hawks books about his sports betting [which he publicly ad-

Dan Horn, "Win or Lose, They Crave the Action: For Addicts Every Day Can Be a Gamble," *The Cincinnati Enquirer*, January 11, 2004. Copyright © 2004 by *The Cincinnati Enquirer*. Reproduced by permission.

mitted to in 2004], millions of Americans like Fred struggle in silence every day with the same destructive compulsion to gamble.

They risk retirement funds, mortgage payments, credit ratings, marriages and even their lives in pursuit of a drug-like high they say they get only from gambling.

Those who study and treat compulsive gamblers estimate that about 6 million to 8 million adults in the United States have serious problems with gambling. Though hard-core gamblers often do not seek help, recent studies suggest their numbers are growing.

The reason is as obvious as the big casino boats docked along Indiana's riverfront: Gambling has never been more available, popular or widely accepted than it is today.

"It's never been that hard to get down a bet," says Keith Whyte, executive director of the National Council on Problem Gambling. "Now it's easier than ever."

Cincinnati proves his point.

The city is an hour's drive from three riverboat casinos. Horse racing is even closer, with tracks in Ohio and Kentucky. Internet gaming is a mouse click away. And lower-stakes games, from church bingo to the state lottery, can be found almost everywhere.

"The game of chance is very much a part of American culture," says Dr. Walter Smitson, director of Cincinnati's Central Clinic, which treats and evaluates mental health disorders.

Billions Won and Lost

It's an expensive one, too. An estimated $900 billion was bet legally in the United States [in 2003].

Most in the gaming industry expect that number to rise as new casinos and online gaming bring high-stakes gambling into every corner of the nation.

"We know it's a problem," says Dr. Susan McElroy, a psychiatry professor at the University of Cincinnati who treats compulsive gamblers. "In general, when you increase access to something that's abuseable, you see an increase in the problem."

A University of Chicago study supports that contention, finding that people gambled more often and spent more money doing it in 1998 than in 1975.

Gambling expenditures had increased from 0.30 percent of personal income to 0.74 percent, and the percentage of adults who had gambled in their lifetime rose from 68 percent to 86 percent.

Other evidence is anecdotal, but researchers say it suggests a growing problem.

The number of weekly Gamblers Anonymous meetings in Greater Cincinnati now stands at 10, double five years ago. The same is true in Kentucky, where some 20 meetings take place each week from Louisville to Lexington.

"There's a growing opportunity for people to gamble," said Mike Stone, director of the Kentucky Council on Problem Gambling. "More people are surfacing for treatment."

Money Problems Grow

A study conducted for lending institutions in 2000 found that bankruptcy rates were an average of 18 percent higher in counties that had casinos or gaming halls than in counties that did not.

Gaming industry officials dispute those findings, saying there are many other causes for America's rising bankruptcy rates. But a bankruptcy trustee in Cincinnati has noticed a change since the riverboat casinos came to Indiana.

"We have seen an increase in the problem," says Eric Goering, who hears bankruptcy cases as a trustee and whose firm handles up to 10 cases a week. He says gambling is a factor in at least 10 percent of bankruptcies.

"Going to the casinos, it's easy to lose $1,000 or $2,000," Goering says. "When you're already living beyond your means, that could put you over the edge."

Gaming industry officials say the problem is not as severe as some make it out to be, but that they're doing their part to help compulsive gamblers.

Ten percent of admission fees at the Indiana boats goes to education and treatment programs for compulsive gamblers. The casinos also post signs urging problem gamblers to call a hot line for help, and they enforce voluntary bans on gamblers struggling to stay away.

"We as an industry take this issue seriously," says Mike Smith, executive director of the Casino Association of Indiana. "I don't know any other industry that does this."

An Intoxicating Effect

Most adults—about 95 percent—have no problem gambling. They can have fun at a casino or bingo hall without risking the kids' college fund.

But those who do have a problem have a significant impact. A federal commission in 1999 estimated that gambling costs the country about $5 billion in bankruptcies, lost productivity and other social costs each year.

"It can affect all areas of life," says McElroy.

She says the definition of a problem gambler is someone who continues to gamble even though it interferes with jobs, relationships and finances. The "action" keeps them coming back for more.

When McElroy asks her patients whether they prefer drugs or gambling, they almost always choose gambling. "The more money someone gambles, the bigger the high," she says. "You're not gambling for fun. You're gambling for the intoxicating effects."

Fred, the former gambler from Northern Kentucky, knows the feeling well. He first felt the thrill while flipping baseball cards and coins as a kid. He soon moved on to horses, sports and casino games.

"We get the excitement from making the bets. That's our drug of choice," Fred says. "It gets to the point where it doesn't matter if you win or lose. It's the action. That's the high."

A Severe Hangover

As with drugs and alcohol, the hangover can be severe.

For years, Fred devoted almost every waking hour to gambling. He owned a business but spent most of his time calling his bookie, playing cards or hanging out at the track.

Eventually, the debt and stress took a toll. He lost his business, his house and his savings. He started having a nightmare in which he was in a casino, losing again and again.

To Fred, suicide seemed the only way to ensure he'd no longer risk his family's money. He says a 30-day stint in a psychiatric hospital and membership in Gamblers Anonymous saved his life.

Other members of Gamblers Anonymous tell similar tales. One says she became "a basket case" as she stole from her husband to feed her addiction to bingo and scratch-off lottery tickets.

Another describes spending night after night at the riverboat casinos, running up credit card debts. "I didn't do anything with my life but work and go to the casino," she recalls. "I didn't buy my grandchildren birthday gifts because all my money had to go to the casino."

A Legitimate Disorder

Experts on problem gambling say they aren't out to ban betting. Even Gamblers Anonymous does not take a position on whether it's inherently good or bad.

What's needed, experts say, is a greater public awareness that compulsive gambling is a serious problem. They want more treatment options, more public education and a greater emphasis on the need to get help before it's too late.

"There's still that barrier there in people's minds toward accepting this as a legitimate disorder," Whyte says. "It hinders efforts to encourage people to seek help."

Whyte and others hope Pete Rose's public struggle will lead to a better understanding of compulsive gambling, even if Rose himself seems unconvinced he has a problem.

More than a decade after he gave up gambling, Fred has no doubt about the seriousness of his problem. He still goes to Gamblers Anonymous meetings, and he still hears the horror stories from gamblers as desperate as he once was.

Not long ago, Fred went to a riverboat casino. He knows he shouldn't have, but some friends wanted to go so he tagged along.

He didn't gamble, but he did see a lot of people who reminded him of his old self.

He recognized the look in their eyes as they played the slots or blackjack. He watched them fight with their spouses over money and rush to the ATM for more cash.

"I could tell the compulsive gamblers," he says. "They can't stop. It's an addiction."

THE GAMING INDUSTRY PROMOTES RESPONSIBLE GAMBLING

Frank J. Fahrenkopf Jr.

The following selection is excerpted from a speech delivered before the Illinois Gaming Board in May 2000. The speaker, Frank
J. Fahrenkopf Jr., is the president and chief spokesperson for the
American Gaming Association (AGA), an industry advocacy organization. Problem gambling is a reality for a small percentage
of the nation's gamblers, Fahrenkopf writes. He also maintains
that the gambling industry is both concerned and affected by
the problems that irresponsible gamblers pose to themselves and
to the gaming community. In fact, Fahrenkopf argues, the gaming industry is committed to addressing problem gambling in an
effort to help those afflicted and to ensure the integrity of the industry. Fahrenkopf claims, for example, that the gaming industry
has poured millions of dollars into research on problem gambling and its treatments. In addition, Fahrenkopf states, the AGA
conducts an educational campaign within the industry to keep
insiders abreast of responsible gaming programs and practices.
The AGA has even worked with the staffs of casinos and other
gambling facilities to teach employees how to spot problem gamblers and intervene on their behalf. In Fahrenkopf's view, the industry's willingness to participate in these programs reveals how
committed it is to curbing problem gambling.

As the [National Gambling Impact Study Commission] reported,
"[T]he vast majority of Americans either gamble recreationally and
experience no measurable side effects related to their gambling, or
they choose not to gamble at all. Regrettably, some of them gamble in
ways that harm themselves, their families, and their communities."
Most of our customers gamble for entertainment and set a budget.
Our research tells us that. However, we recognize that a small percentage of the population cannot gamble responsibly, and we are working
to address that in every way the scientific experts have told us to.

Frank J. Fahrenkopf Jr., "Separating Myth from Fact," speech before the Illinois
Gaming Board, Chicago, IL, May 3, 2000. Copyright © 2000 by the American Gaming Association. Reproduced by permission.

Refuting Unfounded Claims

First, let me say that since our organization was founded [in 1995], we have had a commitment to addressing problem gambling. This has been a commitment in words and deeds, as I will outline later in my remarks.

That said, let me address the topic of the prevalence of pathological gambling. Despite opponents' exaggerated claims as high as 11 percent, we now have the facts before us. Research conducted for the federal commission found that the range of pathological gambling prevalence is somewhere between 0.1 percent and 0.9 percent, according to work by the National Opinion Research Center at the University of Chicago (NORC) and the National Research Council of the National Academy of Sciences (NRC). A 1997 industry-funded study by Harvard Medical School estimated that figure to be 1.29 percent.

Another oft-repeated claim by our opponents is that a high percentage of our revenue comes from pathological gamblers. While some of these unfounded claims have gone as high as 50 percent, I again point you to the commission report's research findings. NORC estimated that 5 percent to 15 percent of the industry's gross revenues were from pathological gamblers. Our companies have said it time and time again. We don't want customers who bet over their heads. We have been working in every way the scientific experts tell us to promote responsible gaming, whether it's educating our customers through posters and brochures, training employees, or posting toll-free help line phone numbers on our casino floors.

Another false charge is that our companies in some way target pathological gamblers in our marketing and that somehow we are able to detect pathological gamblers through our customer database. Ask any treatment expert, and they will tell you that it is impossible for us—or anyone else—to determine who is a pathological gambler based on a list of names and data. In fact, they'll tell you that even in person it is a difficult disorder to diagnose. The experts have told us that our role should be one of educating our employees and customers and funding research—a role that we certainly have undertaken and will continue to do.

Increased Gambling Does Not Lead to Problem Gambling

And now, let me take on the assumption that increased availability of gambling leads to an increase in pathological gambling. While this might seem like a logical assumption, and certainly one perpetuated by our opponents, let me ask you, again, to look at the facts. The first federal gambling commission during the 1970s found that the number of "probable compulsive gamblers" was 0.77 percent of the U.S. adult population, virtually identical to the findings of the latest federal commission, despite the growth of gambling opportunities during that time. As the 1999 federal commission research concluded: "The availability of casinos within driving distance does not appear to affect prevalence rates." Similar government-sponsored research in Minnesota, Texas and Connecticut all showed statistically stable rates of pathological gambling in those states, despite significant increases in the availability of gaming.

If pathological gambling prevalence rates increased along with gambling availability, it would seem logical to see an increased demand for social services in communities with casinos. However, the federal commission's community database analysis found just the opposite: spending on social services was actually lower in places closest to casinos than in places further from casinos.

Another erroneous assumption about our industry is that the more people gamble, the more likely they are to become pathological gamblers. In fact, the NORC research found that while many more people have gambled at least once in their lifetimes (68 percent in 1975, compared to 86 percent in 1999), the number of people who have gambled in the past year has remained relatively unchanged (61 percent in 1975, versus 63 percent in 1999). As the Public Sector Gaming Study Commission pointed out in its final report issued [in 2000], "[T]hese findings mean that Americans have become much more likely to have experimented with gambling, but this experimentation has not turned them into people who gamble regularly or routinely."

Industry Initiatives

As I indicated earlier, the commercial casino industry is committed to working for the development and implementation of education, prevention and treatment programs to address disordered gambling. Our actions have been taken in consultation with the scientific experts, who have told us that our role should be one of educating and funding research to learn more about gambling disorders in order to enhance prevention and treatment methods. Our dedication is demonstrated by our actions, which I'd like to describe for you now.

One of the first initiatives undertaken by the AGA [American Gaming Association] when it was founded in 1995 was to create the National Center for Responsible Gaming (NCRG), an independent organization that funds peer-reviewed research on disordered gambling. The research being conducted by NCRG investigators—at the direction of an advisory board composed of scientific researchers and treatment experts—is helping the scientific community gain a better understanding of the causal factors related to disordered gambling, improve diagnostic methods and identify empirically valid prevention and treatment programs.

Twenty-seven gaming entertainment companies, vendors and suppliers; one foundation; and one union have committed more than $7 million to the National Center. Since it was founded in 1996, the NCRG has awarded 19 grants totaling nearly $2.6 million to respected universities and medical research centers such as Harvard Medical School, Washington University School of Medicine and Massachusetts General Hospital.

I will not go into great detail about the current research being funded by the NCRG, . . . I do think it's important to mention that the National Gambling Impact Study Commission noted that, ". . . the largest source of funding for research on problem and pathological gambling is the casino industry."

Education Campaign

Beyond funding research, the AGA also has developed a comprehensive responsible gaming education program. Let me interject here that these activities are nothing new for the commercial casino industry. Our member companies have a history of encouraging and instituting responsible gaming practices. Harrah's Entertainment, Inc., an operator here in Illinois, pioneered responsible gaming programs more than a decade ago with its two now widely used programs, Operation Bet Smart and Project 21. Since the AGA was formed in 1995, we have built on those programs, spearheading a Responsible Gaming National Education Campaign to encourage the establishment and promotion of responsible gaming practices industrywide.

As a key component of this program, our industry developed and adopted comprehensive, voluntary guidelines to address all aspects of disordered and underage gambling. The AGA also has adopted voluntary guidelines for missing and unattended children, as well as advertising and marketing. The advertising and marketing guidelines are part of an overall program we are developing to ensure appropriate advertising and marketing of casino gaming to adults and avoid content that specifically appeals to children and minors.

The AGA has spearheaded numerous events to focus employee and public attention on this issue. Every year, the first week of August is designated "Responsible Gaming Education Week." During this annual event, companies devote activities to increasing awareness about disordered gambling and the importance of responsible gaming. In 1998, our first year, the week included an AGA-sponsored "Best Ideas" contest for industry employees promoting the education theme. The contest featured several different categories and more than 500 contest entries were received. The winning slogan was included in print materials for last year's Responsible Gaming Education Week: "If you play with real dollars, play with real sense." During each Responsible Gaming Education Week, we have produced and distributed educational brochures relating to this issue for all 250,000 of our casino employees.

The AGA also has conducted seminars on disordered gambling and on responsible gaming programs and practices at the annual World Gaming Congress & Expo, including one on "Understanding Gambling and Its Potential Health Consequences," which was co-sponsored by the National Center for Responsible Gaming, the Nevada Council on Problem Gambling and Harvard Medical School. This same seminar was featured at the Southern Gaming Summit and co-sponsored by the Gulf Coast Gaming Association and the Mississippi Council on Problem Gambling.

Training Casino Employees

In addition, we have conducted responsible gaming certification courses at the World Gaming Congress & Expo. These courses were moderated by experts in the field of disordered gambling and were designed to increase awareness, introduce innovative programs, and further educate casino employees and regulators. We have conducted responsible gaming workshops to provide casino employees with an overview of disordered gambling and responsible gaming programs.

The AGA has developed a variety of print materials intended to teach gaming industry employees about disordered gambling and how the problem should be addressed. These materials include a comprehensive *Responsible Gaming Resources Guide*, which was developed in collaboration with Carl Braunlich of Purdue University and Marvin Steinberg of the Connecticut Council on Compulsive Gambling. The resource guide, which is a collection of industry best practices, is widely used and now in its second edition.

The AGA also has produced the PROGRESS Kit, which includes sample brochures, posters and training curricula. The print materials, all of which are included on a CD-ROM in an electronic file format for customization and printing, address responsible gaming, disordered gambling, underage gambling, cash access in casinos and unattended minors. The curricula, developed for use by gaming industry employees, focus separately on disordered gambling and on underage gambling prevention. These curricula were developed jointly with the North American Training Institute, a division of the Minnesota Council on Compulsive Gambling, and have been certified by the American Academy of Health Care Providers in the Addictive Disorders.

We have collaborated with third parties, including the National Center for Missing and Exploited Children, state problem gambling councils and the Harvard Medical School Division on Addictions, on issues of mutual concern. In this regard, with technical assistance from the National Center, casino employees in Las Vegas, Atlantic City, and the Mississippi Gulf Coast received training on how to respond to cases of unattended children on or outside casino properties, in addition to training through other AGA-sponsored seminars.

A Model to Follow

I might add that our responsible gaming activities have spurred some states to adopt creative new ways to address this problem. In Missouri, for example, the casino industry has forged a diverse coalition involved in the gaming industry in that state to raise public awareness of responsible gaming. The Missouri Alliance to Curb Compulsive Gambling, whose members include the Missouri Riverboat Gaming Association, Missouri Lottery, state department of mental health, Missouri Gaming Commission and Missouri Council on Problem Gambling Concerns, should be a model for other states to follow.

IN DEFENSE OF GAMBLING

Dan Seligman

In the following article journalist Dan Seligman observes that while many Americans claim to hold gambling in contempt, every year millions flock to casinos, play the lottery, and even participate in illegal wagering. Instead of merely accepting gambling as a harmless entertainment, policy makers, Seligman notes, seem to be more concerned with the small percentage of gamblers who cannot control their desire to play. Seligman contends, however, that the few who suffer from problem gambling should not prevent the majority of responsible gamblers from enjoying the experience. Seligman is a respected journalist who had a long career with Time, Inc., but now writes for *Forbes*.

Compulsive gambling is an overrated problem, and the latest research on gamblers suggests we need to rethink it.

A curious thing about gambling in America is that it is extremely popular, yet has a bad reputation—and I don't mean the unsavory way in which gambling licenses are awarded, as described in the preceding story [not included in this viewpoint]. I am talking about the moral realm, as witnessed in the clucking over William Bennett's expensive habit [a story in *Forbes* magazine from June 23, 2003].[1] Casinoland's high rollers are perceived as inhabiting a zone somewhere between immoral and diseased, and have great difficulty defending themselves. Yet in their own lives most Americans demand ever more gambling opportunities. As things stand now [as of June 2003], legal gambling is available in all but three states (Hawaii, Tennessee and Utah), and most Americans admit to gambling sometimes. Surveys done in 1999 for the National Gambling Impact Study Commission told us that 86% of Americans had gambled at some time in their lives, and 68% had gambled within the prior year. Total legal wagering runs around $900 billion a year (about 10% of personal income), of which some $600 billion takes place at casinos. Casinos, long confined to Nevada and New

1. William J. Bennett is a political spokesman and public moralist who served in the administrations of presidents Ronald Reagan and George H.W. Bush. His image as a scourge of public vices, however, was tarnished in 2003 when his penchant for gambling became a media topic.

Dan Seligman, "In Defense of Gambling," *Forbes*, vol. 171, June 23, 2003, pp. 86–88.

Jersey, now also exist in 27 other states (in 15 of which the business is open only to Indians).

That $900 billion covers a broad range of activities, including lotteries, jai alai, pari-mutuel betting on horses and dogs, church and secular bingo, sports betting and more—yet it clearly understates the gambling total. It doesn't include illegal betting, whose total is enormous but unknowable. And it doesn't include the gambling done in America's securities markets by day traders and others. Your broker can perhaps testify to running into customers whose idea of investment is indistinguishable from Las Vegas action. In any event Wall Street offers plenty of bets with risk/reward opportunities that mirror those of slot machines—a long shot with the occasional huge payout. Buying out-of-the-money puts [the option to sell stock at less than current market value] on an airline stock just before a union vote would fall in that category. If the members unexpectedly vote against wage concessions, you could make a killing on the bankruptcy.

Gambling's Evil Image

Despite gambling's broad popularity, its enemies keep coming at it from all directions. To begin with its least influential bad-mouthers, it is generally disfavored by economists. As postulated in several editions of [Harvard professor] Paul Samuelson's famous textbook [of the 1940s, *Foundations of Economic Analysis*], gambling is a bad thing under the principle of diminishing marginal utility. The principle tells us that the $1,000 won on a 999-to-1 bet can buy something less than 1,000 times as much happiness as the dollar put up for the bet. Thus gamblers are collectively losers, even in the idealized lottery, where nothing is taken off the top for overhead and taxes. And, of course, the real world is far from the Platonic ideal—much is lost to overhead.

The other economic formulation has gambling as an evil because it consumes time and resources without creating any new output. You could say the same about climbing Mt. Everest, but somehow economists never weigh in on this front.

What you absolutely never hear from them is that gambling is terrific entertainment, and that perfectly rational people play the lottery and the horses because they get kicks at a price they find reasonable. The price, of course, is not the amount bet but the amount lost by customers succumbing to the vigorish [a charge taken on bets]—the house's edge.

You also don't hear this being acknowledged by people whose livelihood comes from fighting compulsive gambling and who are, therefore, somewhat motivated to exaggerate the problem's magnitude. Gamblers Anonymous, the National Council on Problem Gambling (and its state affiliates), the Compulsive Gambling Center, the International Centre for Youth Gambling Problems, the Chinese Community Problem Gambling Project, Women Helping Women (publishers of a female gambling recovery newsletter) and the Association of Problem Gambling Service Administrators are all out there getting across the message that compulsive gambling is ruining lives. In an average month the Nexis database adds 200 articles mentioning "problem" gambling and 100 or so mentioning "compulsive" gambling.

Everything Has Risk

Yet the overwhelming majority of gamblers are just out there enjoying themselves. The best available—though still flawed—research on the numbers is the study performed several years ago by a panel of the National Academy of Sciences (NAS), which indicated that compulsive gamblers are about 0.9% of the adult population. There is no longer any dispute about the characters in question being seriously self-destructive, as we were reminded recently by the April [2003] obituary of Leonard Tose, who was forced to sell the Philadelphia Eagles to pay $25 million in casino gambling debts. (Charming detail from the *New York Times* obit: It was Lenny's habit to take over blackjack tables and repetitively play seven games simultaneously, at $10,000 apiece.) The NAS says another 2% or so are "problem" gamblers, but this figure is suspect if only because the accompanying definition is so wobbly. A problem gambler is said to be a guy (about two-thirds are male) whose betting "results in any harmful effects" to himself or folks around him. Any harmful effects? Everything you do, from driving cars to taking showers, has some potential for harmful effects.

Possibly you are telling yourself that characters like Leonard Tose do so much damage, to themselves and others, that we must do everything possible to curb the disease, even if its victims are relatively few. It is not clear, however, that we know how to deal with the disease. The National Council on Problem Gambling, one of many organizations that "certifies" counselors to treat problem gamblers, acknowledges that among those who seek counseling, 75% drop out of the programs they are steered to, and only half of the remainder end up abstaining from gambling—an overall success rate of about one-eighth, and this in a group presumed (because they came in voluntarily) to be above average in their motivation.

Perhaps Gambling Is Not the Problem

But the success rate is not the main issue. Recent psychiatric research into compulsive gambling gets into "co-morbidity"—that is, the tendency of problem gamblers to have problems that go beyond gambling. It turns out that alcoholism and drug addiction are rampant among problem gamblers (Tose was an alcoholic), and the NAS study indicates that they also have rates of depression, schizophrenia and "antisocial personality disorder" some three times higher than the rates among nongamblers. All of which raises an interesting question: Is there any such thing as problem gamblers who are otherwise normal? I recently asked this question of Christine Reilly, executive director of the Harvard Medical School's Institute for Pathological Gambling, and she said: "If there is such a group, it's probably a very small group."

Next question: Is it possible that among pathological gamblers, the gambling itself is not really the problem, or at least not the ultimate problem—that it's simply the expression of those other "morbidities"? There are hints in the NAS study that some researchers are close to answering yes to that question, e.g., in a passage indicating drug and alcohol problems are associated with "progression to problem gambling and pathological gambling." And if the answer is affirmative, it would seem to follow that we wouldn't really get very far by limiting gambling opportunities. There are, after all, plenty of other ways for drunks and drug addicts to ruin their own and their families' lives.

CHAPTER 5

GAMBLING STORIES

THE DOWNSIDE OF WINNING THE LOTTERY

Pam Lambert et al.

For many people winning the lottery would be a miraculous event that would mean an end to worry and an opportunity to enjoy the good life. In the following article Pam Lambert and fellow staff writers at *People* magazine explore true-life tales of lottery winners whose postjackpot lives did not turn out as bright as they had hoped. In fact, as the authors report, some of these winners lost their newfound wealth as quickly as they had won it; others found the sudden riches to be more of a burden than a salvation.

Millions of Americans daydream about hitting a megamillion jackpot—and assume all that's left is to live happily ever after. Could happen. Or—as these unlucky *lottery* winners show—a sudden windfall can also lead to divorce, bankruptcy and (gulp) even hit men.

Jay Sommers, [Age] 36, Won: $5.8 Million

Outcome: Lost It All, Delivered Pizza

Oh, to be young, handsome and suddenly so rich you can outshop Paris Hilton! Jay Sommers was 20 when he won a fifth of a $28.9 million lottery jackpot in Michigan in 1988. With his first annual $290,000 payment he bought not one but five new cars. "I blew all of the check in 2½ months," says Sommers. "What 20-year-old wins that kind of money and is sensible with it?"

Oh, to be young, handsome and suddenly so broke you're delivering pizza! Spending so fast he couldn't pay taxes, Sommers asked a friend who is a businessman to manage his loot. His pal persuaded Sommers to swap his annual checks for a discounted lump-sum payout. One day in the mid-'90s Sommers went to the bank and discovered all his money was gone—frittered away by his friend's bad investments and shady deals. Sommers sued his friend and won the case, but spent much of his $887,000 settlement paying off lawyers and debts. To make ends meet during the case he took the pizza-delivery job. "People recognized me and it was humiliating" says Sommers, 36. "One minute I'm famous and five years later I'm broke. It's been a roller coaster ride."

Single and living near Detroit, Sommers now does construction

Pam Lambert et al., "The High Cost of Winning," *People*, vol. 61, March 15, 2004, pp. 150–53. Copyright © 2004 by Time, Inc. Reproduced by permission.

work and is a racecar driver trying to make it big in NASCAR. "I'm still bitter and I'll be bitter the rest of my life," he says. "I think I'd be further along today if I had never won."

Callie Rogers, 17, Won: $3.5 Million

Outcome: Lost Fiancé, Peace of Mind

After supermarket clerk Callie Rogers, then 16, bagged her jackpot [in] June [2003], "I just sat there crying," the British teen recalls. Over the coming months there would be more tears in store. First, jealousy reared its ugly head. "People I didn't know were saying bad things about me," she says. Then her 25-year-old boyfriend proposed—and told her she'd have to buy her own ring, promising to pay her back. She ended up dumping him. "I knew he was a loser before I got rich," she says now.

These days things are looking brighter for Rogers. She has a new, live-in boyfriend, 24-year-old Nicky Lawson. "He's got his own money," Rogers says. "He bought me my ring."

Andrew "Jack" Whittaker, 56, Won: $314.9 Million

Outcome: Embarrassing Busts, Stolen Bucks

As Andrew "Jack" Whittaker should be able to attest, tippling and toting around large stashes of cash don't make for a winning ticket. Since bagging the largest single Powerball jackpot ever on Christmas Day, 2002, a lump-sum windfall of $113.4 million after taxes, the married contractor from Scott Depot, W.Va., has survived a series of misadventures that sound like something from *The Sopranos*. [Since mid-2003] Whittaker, 56, has been drugged at a strip club and robbed of $545,000 (it was recovered); arrested for threatening to have a bar manager and his family killed (he faces a March [2004] court date); and charged with drunk driving after state police found him sitting in his Cadillac SUV on the side of the interstate on Jan. 25, allegedly slumped over the wheel with the vehicle running. Said Whittaker, whose blood-alcohol level registered 0.190, twice the legal limit: "I wasn't driving, absolutely wasn't driving."

Many locals seem inclined to view Whittaker's troubles tolerantly, however, especially since he earmarked $14 million to establish a foundation that delivers food, clothing and scholarships to the state's poor. "I just keep on doing what I'm doing," Whittaker said after his DUI arrest, "and tell everyone my personal life is my own business."

Billie Bob Harrell Jr., 50, Won: $31 Million

Outcome: Lost His Marriage—and His Life

Billie Bob Harrell Jr. was just about broke when he played the Texas Lotto Jackpot in June 1997. But then six ping-pong balls landed the right way and Harrell, 48, was $31 million richer. He quit his job at Home Depot and with his first $1.24 million check took his family to Hawaii, gave tens of thousands to his church, lavished cars and houses on friends and family. He even bought 480 turkeys for the poor. "He played Santa Claus," says his mother, Agnes. "He seemed to think everything would be all right. But it never was the same again."

Suddenly strangers were calling demanding donations; Harrell changed his phone number several times. The strain of it all damaged his marriage, and less than a year after winning Harrell split from his wife. Reckless spending and lending led him to make a bad deal with a company that gives lottery winners lump-sum payments in exchange for their annual checks, and Harrell wound up with much less than what he had won. But by then, it seemed, all he wanted was to have his family back. One night in 1999, just before he was set to meet his ex-wife for dinner, his oldest son found him dead of a shotgun wound. "Winning the lottery," Harrell had earlier told a friend, "was the worst thing that ever happened to me."

Today Harrell's mother does not believe her son took his own life, despite a police report ruling it a suicide. In the bedroom that night police found a note they believe was meant for his ex-wife. "I didn't want this," Harrell wrote. "I just wanted you."

Denise Rossi, 53, Won: $1.3 Million

Outcome: Stripped of Her Winnings

Blindsided—that's how Thomas Rossi felt when Denise, his wife of 26 years, hit him with divorce papers in 1997. "I thought we got along good," says Rossi, 70, a photographer. "I couldn't understand it. She wanted me to move out of the house very fast. It wasn't like her to act this way."

Two years later it all made sense. A letter addressed to his ex-wife that mistakenly arrived in his new Los Angeles apartment revealed she had won a lottery. Rossi learned Denise had scored $1.3 million in the California lottery on Dec. 28, 1996—11 days before she filed for divorce. He took her to court for not disclosing the money, and the judge awarded Rossi the entire haul. According to her lawyer Connolly Oyler, Denise could have kept half and perhaps all of her loot had she been honest, but the court ruled "her failure to disclose was a fraud," he says. Since then Denise has disappeared (she could not be located for comment), but not before trashing Rossi. "I was very happy to be free of this person that was like a parasite," she told NBC's *Dateline* in 2000. "[Winning the lottery] has brought me really nothing but grief and headache."

Receiving $48,000 after taxes every year, meanwhile, has given Rossi "peace of mind," he says. "If it wasn't for the lotto, Denise and I would probably still be together. Things worked out for the best."

William Post, 64, Won: $16.2 Million

Outcome: Brother Hired a Hit Man to Kill Him, Divorce, Bankruptcy

Gone are the days when William Post, 64, would find a pair of pants he liked and buy 400 of them. Gone too are the mansion, the farm, the half-dozen cars and the diamonds. In fact, looking around Post's ramshackle home in Franklin, Pa., you'd never suspect that 16 years ago he won $16.2 million. And yet despite declaring bankruptcy in 1994 and suffering from health problems including severe asthma, Post maintains, "I'm a very happy man now. Money can't buy peace of mind."

As an overnight multimillionaire, that was certainly something that eluded the onetime circus cook. In 1994 his brother Jeffrey pleaded no contest to hiring a hit man to kill Post and his then wife, Connie, allegedly in order to get his hands on Post's estate. (Jeffrey is serving 20 years probation.) Spooked by the plot, Connie left Post not long after. From there things deteriorated further, in large part because of Post's lavish and sometimes bizarre spending sprees. "As soon as the stores opened he'd want to go and buy stuff," says his daughter Gladys Burrous, 42. "Everything, anything."

Today Post lives on a $558 monthly Social Security disability check and has $43 in the bank. "He probably is happier," says Burrous of her father. "When he won, he really didn't know how to handle it."

HOPING TO WIN AT BINGO

Dan Washburn

Though not as exciting as brightly lit casinos, bingo halls still maintain a devoted clientele that is mostly made up of older Americans who cannot afford to travel great distances to gamble. High-stakes Indian bingo is quite popular with this crowd, but as Dan Washburn reports in the following article, charitable organizations such as the Elks Club in Gainesville, Georgia, can still attract loyal gamblers who seem satisfied to win jackpots as low as sixteen dollars. No matter what the stakes, Washburn observes, bingo players are a unique breed who carry totems and stage customary rituals in the hope that such small measures will put the odds in their favor. Dan Washburn is a sportswriter for the *Times*, a Gainesville, Georgia, newspaper.

When Bernie Olejnik took his seat behind the Bingo King Autotronic 7600, everybody shut up. Many in the crowd of nearly 100 at the Gainesville Elks Lodge on Sunday had been waiting more than an hour for this moment—waiting patiently for that first bright numbered ball to separate itself from the pack, waiting for the bingo to begin.

They arrive early for a reason, I learned. There are lucky seats to be secured, lucky trinkets to arrange on the table. Bingo players are constantly trying to change the course of chance.

And each game, one or two of them do. There's always a winner in bingo. That's how the game sucks you in.

Olejnik didn't have to call out many numbers for me to remember why as a child I used to spend so much time in the bingo tents at the Bloomsburg Fair back in Pennsylvania.

I used to plunk my quarter down and play, anxious to win something, anything. Perhaps some plastic mixing bowls or a set of steak knives. I rarely had any use for the prizes, but I always found winning to be wonderful.

The bingo cards at the fair were thick and worn on the edges. We used peanuts as markers.

Compared to bingo at the Gainesville Elks, that old set-up seems like, well, peanuts.

Cards are slick sheets of paper and used only once. Plastic bottles full of ink, known as "dobbers," make the marks. Some players even tote their personal dobber collections around in hand-knit carrying cases.

Prizes given away every Sunday at the Elks made the steak knives of my youth seem rather silly.

Nine games pay out $1,100, $600 of which is for a single game known as the "jackpot." The Elks, actually, would like to offer more prize money, but Georgia law won't allow it.

"We can't do near what the Indians can do up in North Carolina," said Ron Harlan, former Elks exalted ruler and current chairman of the bingo committee. "That does cut into our business a bit. The real avid players will go up there."

Still, the Elks take in around $1,500 from bingo each weekend. That's enough to keep several charities happy.

And the stakes are high enough to keep a rather large crowd of regulars coming back each week.

Max and Marion Paton, who raise breeding chickens on their farm in Dawsonville, rarely miss a Sunday afternoon of bingo. Max is 82. Marion is 80. They'll be married 59 years in April.

"Oh yeah, we have a lot of fun," said Max, a World War II veteran. "We enjoy it. This is like entertainment."

"And," Marion offered, "they do as a whole have very nice people here."

Added Max, "You don't get a bunch of fibbers."

The Patons always try to grab the table that straddles the barrier between the smoking and non-smoking rooms. They don't care for the smoke—and there is plenty (you should smell my clothes)—but they also don't like to be out of view of the Bingo King Autotronic 7600, either.

And the Bingo King Autotronic 7600 sits in the smoking room, because that's where most of the bingo players sit. The two habits seem to go hand in hand.

The Bingo King Autotronic 7600 looks like something out of a 1960s sci-fi movie, like one of those handwriting analysis machines you find at local carnivals.

Through the machine's window, you can watch the bingo balls toss about, and get sucked to the top one by one. Where the balls pop out, a video camera awaits. The current ball is broadcast to several televisions positioned throughout the bingo room.

Then Olejnik makes the call. "Next number. Under the 'O.' Sixty-four. That's 'O' six-four." The number lights up on the big board behind Olejnik and the Bingo King Autotronic 7600.

This is definitely not the Bloomsburg Fair.

But the game still plays the same. You still need your numbers to be called. You still need them to occupy the right combination of squares on your card.

They didn't for Max. "I'll be a son of a gun," he said again and again. "They're all in the wrong places."

But they did for Marion. Olejnik called out "I 28" and Marion called out "Bingo!" So did several others. They each won $16.70.

Anticipation and Excitement

You can tell when a game of bingo is coming to a close. The crowd senses it. With each number called, anticipation grows. You feel your time is running out. There is a murmur. Then there is a winner.

"I get very excited when I win," said Joyce Head, 55, of Murrayville. "It's like a shot. I mean really, it's like one. It is."

Head "gave up smoking and took up bingo" several years ago. One can be as addictive as the other. On Saturday, Head headed up to Rock Hill, S.C., for some high stakes bingo. She didn't win, but said she knows she will again soon. She likes to think of her bingo card as half full, not half empty.

"I go expecting to win," Head said. "I mean you've got to be there. You can't win sitting at home."

How about sitting on a horseshoe? B.T. Hudgins does that.

"Anything to help out," the Gainesville resident said. Hudgins and friend Jean Bachelor also carry around buckeyes in their pockets for luck.

Others will place troll dolls, four-leaf clovers or other knickknacks before them for good fortune. Elephant figurines are supposed to work, too . . . but only if the trunk is pointing up.

Some feel the only way to increase the chance of winning is to increase the number of bingo cards. I watched one lady play 39 at once. I had enough trouble with six.

Betty Ladewig, a 74-year-old from Murrayville, had 27 cards in front of her and nothing else. She doesn't believe in good luck charms.

And she won one of the $600 prizes last week.

"I think it's all dumb luck," she said. "But I like to gamble."

Perhaps I do, too, Betty. I'd think I got my 10 dollars' worth of excitement on Sunday.

One time I was a "B 2" and a "B 9" from winning $100. I felt a rush overtake my body.

Then again, maybe it was just the cigarette smoke.

GAMBLING IS ALL ABOUT LUCK

Anonymous, interviewed by Robert O'Malley

Robert O'Malley is a writer, editor, and photographer living in Massachusetts. He brought *Sampan* magazine, a New England journal of Asian American culture, to the Internet. In the following article from *Sampan*, O'Malley interviews an unnamed gambler from the Asian American community. According to the interviewee, successful gamblers know how to gauge their own luck. The woman maintains that she has been very fortunate gambling, but says that she knows when her luck has run out. She claims that she always brings a set amount of gambling money to a casino and keeps in mind that she has a family to support. Playing mah-jongg, blackjack, or any other game of chance makes her feel good, she observes. She also believes that any money she loses will eventually return to her when her luck returns.

When I first started gambling I used to play mah jongg at home. Playing mah jongg gave me a chance to meet with friends. Every time I played I could also bring the kids together. I have kids and my friends have kids, so the kids could play together while the mothers were playing. Sometimes I'd get lucky and win some money. This made me happy. At home I didn't lose much.

In the beginning I'd gamble about $20. In the beginning it was very very small. Sometimes if I had bad luck I would lose $50 to $100 at home, but mostly I'd win or lose $50. I like playing mah jongg because I can control it and not risk too much. If it's a small game I won't get much money but I won't lose much either. If you play a big game you can win more money but it's hard to win.

I Love Casinos

When Atlantic City opened I started to go there. I would get there by bus or by car. In the beginning I liked the slot machines, but I'd lose a lot of money in them. Most of the time I'd lose like a few hundred. If I went to Atlantic City I'd have at least $1000 in my pocket. Most of the time I'd lose all of it; I wouldn't leave until there wasn't even a cent left in my pocket. Of course I would feel upset, but I couldn't control myself. I liked the fun of it. When you hit the jackpot, the money comes out of the machine and it sound so good. If I can win the money I don't feel bored.

I love casinos! I like them because you only see people gambling, walking around and playing there. The rooms have a lot of light. It makes me feel happy. I never know if it's dark or light, daytime or night-time outside. I don't have to worry about outside. Inside the casino, you see people 24 hours.

After I lost $2000 or $3000 at Atlantic City one night, I felt scared. After going there about seven times, I said I wouldn't go there anymore. The trip made me feel tired because I needed to ride on the bus for seven hours. This was maybe six or seven years ago. After that I gambled only at home. I played mah jongg. I started to play a little bit bigger then. Now I usually play a few hundred dollars a night.

I am interested in any kind of gambling. I either go somewhere in my neighborhood or to my friend's home . . . which is quiet and comfortable. I tell myself that that is a very good place to play mah jongg. Why? Because the table we play on is so special and my friends treat me very good. She cooks for us. So we just eat and gamble. She's a good cook. We have coffee. Almost every week I go to her home to play. We play from Friday night until Saturday, or from Saturday night until Sunday. I like to play a long time—all night. We play maybe 16 hours, from Saturday at 3 o'clock to Sunday at 12 o'clock. We don't sleep at all. We don't get tired until the end, and then we go home and sleep. I'm happy to play. Of course we get upset if we lose but we get upset with the game, not with the people. This week the money goes to you, but next week it comes back to me.

Luck and Skill

I started going to Foxwoods [a popular casino in Connecticut] in 1997. I go there at least once or twice a week. In the beginning I didn't bet when I went there. Then after about the fifth or sixth time I started to bet. Then I got crazy. I wanted to go whenever I had a chance. My friend drives me there. It's so easy to get on the bus to go, but I would rather drive because then I don't have to be controlled by the time. It's easy to drive down. Any time I feel like it I can just go. On Saturdays I like to go after dinner, after I settle down from everything. Most of the time I leave at about 7:30 and get there at 9 o'clock. I stay till Sunday. When I play I don't need to sleep. I don't want to leave. I get on the Black Jack table. First thing I do is take a look at the different tables. If there's a seat I just sit down and play.

First I take out $100 to play a small game. When you gamble first you need luck, then you need some skill. It's exciting when I get lucky. Every time I hit a good game I ask for the good cards. If I ask for a good card it's more exciting. I can't tell beforehand if I'm going to have good luck or bad luck. I only know that I feel good when I have money in my pocket because it means I have a chance to bet. I go in with at least $500 or $1,000; if I have more I will take more. I don't set aside special money for gambling.

One time I went to Foxwoods with only $100. I hit the jackpot! I was so happy. It was a slot machine. I just put the money in and played the slot machine. $2,500 came out. That was at the end of March. Because I had only $100 I didn't want to sit at the Black Jack table. At the Black Jack table I need more than $100 to play.

Last week I got really lucky—on big games and small games, at home and at Foxwoods. I won because of the feng shui. A few weeks ago a fortuneteller told me to move the clock from the wall beside me to the back wall. Two people helped me do that. After I moved the clock I got lucky.

This weekend I got so lucky. More than lucky! I had a lot of fun at the Black Jack table. I went to Foxwoods on Saturday. I left home at 7 o'clock with my friend and coworker. We got there at about 9 o'clock and went to separate places to play. I went to play Black Jack.

At first I had very bad luck. I lost the money I brought—$1,000. I don't know how long I was gambling because I don't carry a watch. After I lost I went to look for my friend. I said "Let me have $100." And he gave it to me—$100 in chips. In my purse I also had an extra $75. So I sat down and bet $25. On weekends they don't have small tables.

So I started with $25 and lost the $75 I had in my purse. So I told myself, "I don't have luck. Why not bet one time? Because if I bet $25 I can't make money." So I put the whole $100 down, and I won that game. I won $100—one to one. So then I doubled down and I won again, so I got $300. So that meant I had $400. So I doubled down again and I hit it. I had $800. I was so happy! I said I must go. I wanted to go but I said, "No, I've got luck." So that's why I kept playing more and more. So I took back $600 and I bet $200. But I was lucky and I won more and more. So I don't know how long I sat at that table, but I made $4,000. I don't know how much time I needed. Of course I took back $1,000 of my money so that meant I only made $3,000. I felt so happy; I thought, "I should go." But I said, "I still have luck because the dealer is so good to me. This is my lucky night." So that's why I kept playing. And so I kept playing and somehow I lost $1,500. And then I left. I had at least a $2,000 profit.

Then I met someone who lost all her money. I know that woman. Yeah she's from Chinatown. She asked me, "How did you do?" I said, "I made some." And she asked me to lend her $100. I said, "$100 is not enough to bet, maybe you need $200." And then she said, okay, she would return it to me. She said she had lost, like, $4,000. Every time I go there I see her.

This weekend when I was at the table an old Chinese woman came up to me; she was over 70 years old. She wanted me to buy a coupon from her. She came by bus and got the coupon with her ticket. I don't know where she came from. She maybe saw I was Chinese. So she asked me to buy the coupon from her. She had five coupons, which are worth $10 each. Everybody who takes the bus gets a coupon. To use the coupon you have to bet an equal amount of your own money. She didn't want to bet because she didn't know if she could get back the money. It would be safer for her if she just sold me the coupon. She said she would give me $20 for five coupons. So I said, "Okay, I'll give you $50." And she was very very happy. Usually they don't get that lucky. Maybe because of this I got lucky too.

Keeping It Affordable

I see a lot of people from Chinatown at Foxwoods; most of the time I see the same faces. Yes, some people lose a lot of money. But for me, I can still control myself because I have a family to take care of. I'm not really really crazy. I'm crazy but I'm not really really crazy. I work every day.

Some people who lose a lot sometimes lose their house or their restaurant. I know a friend who lost his restaurant. He had to run away so he wouldn't be tempted. He moved to another state because he wanted to be far away from Foxwoods. It's too easy to get to Foxwoods—only two hours. He lost everything. Even some people lose their family. I don't know why they do it. Gambling is too interesting; gambling makes it very easy for you to do something crazy.

I like to gamble because if you get lucky you can make some easy money. If you don't get lucky you lose. That's why I don't bring my credit card; I don't bring my bank card; I only take the money I can afford to lose. Before I used to bring my bank card. It was so easy to get money. If I lost, I would say, "Okay, get some money." That's why I don't bring the card. Some people bring a bank card, credit card, whatever they can. I think the Chinese like to gamble about as much as everybody else.

When I gamble I don't feel tired; I don't feel sleepy. If I have money I feel happy to gamble; you don't even know the time is passing. Of course if I win my kids are happy and I'm happy. But if I lose money . . .

If I stay at home too much my kids will say, "Mom, how come you don't gamble?" They will say that because they know I'm interested in gambling more than anything else.

I think it's up to the person if she wants to gamble or not. If they want to do it they do it. At least they don't kill people or rob people. I don't think it's bad. Some people like to travel but I don't like to travel. Travel makes me very tired, but some people enjoy travel. It's just like that: different people, different types. I think if you lose a restaurant, that's too much. If I say, "Today I can lose $1000," then I bring $1,000. That's all. If I get lucky I can bring home more than $1,000.

Nonjudgmental Community

I will share my luck, my happiness with everybody, with my family and my friends. I will buy gifts for my kids. I will do something I want to do. I like Foxwoods because at Foxwoods all the people are the same. They're all gambling people. So I don't have to worry about people saying, "Oh, you do bad; you gamble a lot." Because we're the same type of people. I think this is interesting for me because I don't have to worry about someone saying, "How come you don't go to school? How come you don't go to work? Something like that. Because we are in the same building.

I like casinos because the lights are on 24 hours; you don't need to turn off the lights early. In the casino, it's always like daytime, always the same. When I sit at the table I just concentrate on the table.

When luck comes it just comes. When you hit the game you feel strange. Black Jack is difficult. You have to think, "Do I ask for a card or not?" If you have 17 you can stay, but if you have 12 to 16 it's very hard to ask for a card because you could lose right away. So you're thinking.

Maybe if you have luck you don't have to worry about anything. You just ask for the card, and you will get a good card that fits you.

THE RUIN OF A BASEBALL STAR

Fred Girard

In the following article Fred Girard, a reporter for the *Detroit News*, details how problem gambling helped ruin the lives of former Detroit Tigers, and later New York Yankees, baseball player Cecil Fielder and his family. As Girard reports, Fielder, who retired from the game with salary earnings of $47 million, became infamous after losing over $500,000 in just one day of casino gambling. As Girard implies, that unlucky day was not unique in Fielder's betting life. His wife Stacey had known about her husband's problem but remained ignorant of its extent. She ended up filing for divorce when the family's income disappeared in gambling debts and failed investments.

Detroit just loved Cecil Fielder, the burly Tigers slugger who ushered in the Decade of the Home Run in the early 1990s.

And Detroiters loved Fielder the family man, who doted on his son, Prince, and daughter, Ceclynn. They applauded when wife Stacey was named Mrs. Michigan, posing for pictures in her elegant Grosse Pointe Farms home.

Their storybook life seemed headed for the happiest of endings—Fielder was traded to the Yankees, eventually retired with career earnings of $47 million in salary alone, and moved his family to the largest, richest mansion in central Florida.

Now, it's all gone.

All the money, the mansion—even the loving family unit.

Fielder is in hiding, with process servers stalking him. He is not in contact with his family, and many attempts by *The Detroit News* to reach him failed.

Why?

"Gambling caused Cecil Fielder's empire to collapse," said Al Arostegui, the Realtor who sold the Fielders their 50-room palace in Melbourne, Fla., in 1995 for $3.7 million.

"This isn't a story of a hero who went bad, but a hero who got sick. For Cecil, gambling is a disease; it's like a cancer of some sort that ate away his wealth."

Arostegui said he is owed more than $70,000 by the Fielders in unpaid advertising expenses from his attempts to sell their house for them. Still, he says, "The biggest losers are the Fielders themselves. They had a great dream home, a wonderful life, and now it's all gone."

Stacey Fielder said she still loves her husband, the only man in her life since her early teens, even though the two are mired in a bitter divorce dispute.

"But this isn't the same Cecil," she said. "I never saw any of this coming. I never even knew he gambled."

Sickness Starts Small

By the time Cecil made his first halting admissions to her that he had a problem, she says, their home had been foreclosed on by a bank, and a string of lawsuits and liens worth millions had been filed by creditors.

She is hard up financially and looking for work, she says, and she and Ceclynn, now 12, receive no money from Fielder and don't even have medical insurance.

No one interviewed by *The News* had an inkling that Fielder may have become a heavy gambler.

Fielder "never showed that side around me or any of his friends," said Tigers third base coach Juan Samuel, who has been close to Fielder for 20 years. "A lot of times it starts small, a little bet here and there, maybe even in the clubhouse—before you know, things get out of hand."

The origins of the Fall of the House of Fielder are spelled out in a file in New Jersey Superior Court, titled Trump Plaza Hotel and Casino versus Cecil G. Fielder. It's about one 40-hour period in which Fielder's gambling compulsion apparently broke all bounds, with a casino extending him credit every step of the way.

On a February day in 1999, Cecil Fielder walked into the Trump Plaza casino in Atlantic City just before noon, and filled out an application for credit.

Under "Income/Assets," he included: "Salary—$5 million."

Under "Other Casinos," he listed a $100,000 line of credit at the Desert Inn in Las Vegas.

Trump extended Fielder a $25,000 line of credit. That money, plus whatever cash he had started with, lasted a day and a half.

Fielder requested, and was given, another $25,000 line of credit.

That was gone in two hours and 40 minutes.

The casino lent him $27,500 more.

That lasted less than 20 minutes.

The casino extended Fielder's credit by another $50,000.

The minute-by-minute records stop there, but the file contains a total. By the time the binge was over, Fielder owed the Trump casino $580,000.

Fielder repaid some small amounts, but held off Trump's collectors on the bulk of the money until September 2000. On the 9th, he wrote a personal check to Trump Plaza for $300,000, and authorized his bank to pay a half-dozen more drafts for $25,000 each.

The next day, Fielder authorized four more drafts from his bank, totaling $130,000. Fielder stopped payment on his personal $300,000 check. The 10 bank drafts all bounced for insufficient funds.

A spokesman for the New Jersey State Police Gaming Enforcement Division said they investigated the transactions, but determined no criminal conduct had occurred.

Trump Plaza Associates sued and won, but has yet to collect. With interest and attorney's fees, the bill stands at $563,359. . . .

"I never knew anything about any of this until I started noticing things when I was doing the finances," Stacey Fielder said. "I'd be going over the bills with the accountant, and I'd be like, 'Hey, there's $35,000 gone from this account. What happened to it?' Then these gambling people just descended on the house one day, and started just taking things out of it. They took my truck.

"We talked about it (Cecil's gambling) only a few times. I was under the impression he was going to get some help."

Sins of the Father

Life became a swirl of lawsuits, process servers, bounced checks, lien after lien filed against their property—and not even the children were spared.

As Prince Fielder, then a husky, 18-year-old first-baseman for the Class A Beloit (Wis.) Snappers, trotted off the field after a home game one day in August 2002, a man stepped out from behind the bleachers to intercept him. It wasn't a reporter or fan. It was a process server, who for months had been searching for his dad, who was living with his son at the time. The man shoved some papers into Prince Fielder's hands, naming his father as defendant in a $387,744 lawsuit.

Although Prince Fielder wasn't a defendant in the suit, the sins of the father—poor business decisions and an unstoppable gambling compulsion—had been visited upon the son, in the form of an extremely embarrassing incident.

"Oh, my God, this is the first time I'm hearing that story," Stacey Fielder said. "That's just another thing I was kept in the dark about."

Prince Fielder declined to be interviewed. . . .

Fielder isn't reachable either, several lawyers interviewed by *The News* said.

"Needless to say, it's been a challenge to track Mr. Fielder down. He's been very elusive," said Madison, Wis., attorney Robert Fleischacker—the man who took the extraordinary step of having Fielder's son served after several other attempts had failed.

Fleischacker said he also dispatched a process server to find Fielder at the baseball All-Star Game in Houston this year, but, "We weren't quick enough on the draw."

The Fielders' divorce case is dragging on as well, because lawyers representing Cecil Fielder don't get paid, then withdraw from the case, according to Stacey Fielder's attorney, Lawrence Banigan of Mineola, N.Y.

"It's like wrestling in a fog," he said.

LOSING EVERYTHING ON THE SLOTS

Nadine Lawton

Nadine Lawton is a pseudonym for a Toronto, Canada, woman who penned the following story for the *Toronto Star* newspaper. Lawton claims that gambling became a disastrous addiction for her. In just two years, Lawton reports, she lost $150,000 to casino slot machines. A real estate agent by trade, Lawton states that she was able to hide her addiction from friends and associates. Her debts became so overwhelming, however, that she started skipping work, writing bad checks, and even contemplated robbing a convenience store. Lawton believes that her problem gambling was a reaction to stresses in her life. She eventually found help in an addiction treatment center and has since taken on other responsibilities in her life to fill time and keep her from the temptation of returning to the slots.

Gambling is a current affair in Ontario. But not with me. Not any more.

My four-year affair with the insidious disease ended recently, but long after it had ruined me in every way imaginable.

Just the way it's ruining others right this minute.

The Star's recent series on problem gamblers could have been written about me and any of the countless others who find themselves in thrall to slot machines, video lottery terminals, blackjack tables, poker machines.

More people than we know are addicted to gambling—writing bad cheques, lying, stealing, skipping work—all to feel the high of instant gratification. But unlike other addictions, it's often hidden. There's no weaving gait or slurred speech; no needle tracks.

For three years, none of my friends knew I gambled. I went alone, and usually late at night. Playing the slots—as often as possible, and at any cost—was my Number 1 obsession.

When I finally woke up, I found myself $30,000 in debt. When I sat down and did the math, I found the casinos had scooped $150,000 of my hard-earned—and borrowed—money in just two years.

How did it happen? A few months ago, I lay in bed pondering that question with a tight stomach and a desperate feeling. I had been a

Nadine Lawton, "Everything to Lose," *Toronto Star*, January 8, 2005. Copyright © 2005 by Toronto Star Newspapers Limited. Reproduced by permission of the author.

star in my workplace, had won an award for outstanding achievement in my field in 2003. I'm an urban professional with my own home; I had good friends and close family.

Why had a machine become my lover, best friend and confidante for so long? Because, I finally realized, gambling was my escape route from troubling times, thoughts, stresses. "Organized chaos" is a term I and others use to describe how potential addicts live, on the slippery slope: busy, productive highs and desperate lows, with not much in between.

It used to be that, when the lows got to me, I would go to a film or visit the gym or call a friend. Then I got hooked on the slots, the "crack cocaine" of gambling. The casino became an alternative to (what seemed like) burdening friends, family or lovers with the latest drama.

I was a winner early on—at first. It was when I started losing but kept on gambling that I realized it wasn't about the money. I would head to the slots for any reason, good or bad. And I missed out on life: parties, functions, the gym, morning coffee with friends.

The lying was masterful, particularly the lying to myself.

The first notable sign of trouble was when I started turning down work. I was freelancing, so there was no answering to anyone, no boss to manipulate. But when the gambling got so bad that I had to pawn my one possession of value, the essential tool of my trade—my $3,500 camera outfit—I decided to 'fess up.

The few friends and family I told were shocked. I'd always been focused, frugal, disciplined in my spending, earning the nickname Bargain Betty.

Whatever snapped, four years ago, the result was the antithesis of how I'd always led my life.

The small circle that knew my problem tried to help. They suggested Gamblers Anonymous, but I squirmed through my first meeting and fled when it was over. "I can control this myself," I'd said as I drove home. Shortly thereafter, I had to cash in my RRSPs [registered retirement savings plan], a few stocks and all my savings. All my earnings went to support my habit.

A Life in Decline

Around this time I completed my studies and got my real estate licence. I did very well in my first year and the large commissions were like all my Christmases had come at once. With my new status as a high-income earner, I was eligible for a line of credit and an overdraft.

Meanwhile, my personal life went to pot.

My partner, who had been more than generous and supportive, finally insisted I join the self-exclusion program the gambling industry runs for addicts—essentially, banning myself from casinos. I enrolled but quickly reneged, returning to the slots even though I could have been charged with trespassing had I been caught.

The insanity became all-consuming. My mind reeled with ideas of how to get money, where to get it from and how I'd get it back to whoever lent it to me. In desperation, I started to write bad cheques.

Through it all, miraculously, I managed to seem "normal" to most people. I had grown up in an alcoholic home where secrets were well-kept. I think now that my success at hiding my addiction stemmed from that early training.

Finally, the merry-go-round shuddered to a halt. My partner and I broke up. I had been unable to cover a cheque and got the dreaded call from my bank. And a therapist I'd been seeing for other issues discontinued treatment when I told him I couldn't pay him that particular week.

"Then I can't see you," he said, taking a deep breath. "Not until you give up gambling."

Not only had I finally been told No, but also, for the first time in a long time I'd actually felt the blow. This was the turning point that led me back to Gamblers Anonymous.

Finding Help

Either I saw it through different eyes, or I was different. I was ready for it and understood that yes, I did belong there. Yes, I could not do this alone. Yes, I was out of control.

It was at this meeting I met John B. His story was a nightmare. After hearing it, I felt brave and told mine. He approached me at the break. When I told him the shape I was in and was considering bankruptcy, he gave me a number to call.

John's contact was a bankruptcy trustee, who was very understanding. Most of his clients claiming bankruptcy in the last five years were compulsive gamblers who had lost everything, he said.

He is anticipating an epidemic. "You ain't seen nothin' yet," he said when I left.

"Why had a machine become my lover, best friend and confidante for so long?"

In the end, I was able to avoid bankruptcy, but just. In my business, it would be a "fate worse than debt."

Even more important, I was able to get help for my gambling addiction.

I'd heard about Homewood Health Centre in Guelph [in Ontario Province] and its 28-day residential program for addicts but knew it had a two-year waiting list. I knew I couldn't wait, but John B. had told me about Homewood's outpatient program. I was lucky to get into the program straight away, and my sister in Guelph was willing to put me up (or should I say, put up with me!).

"If you can't control it, are preoccupied with doing it and do it despite the negative consequences, you're an addict," says Homewood director Dr. Graeme Cunningham. This is what I learned Day 1 of my stay at the 'Wood.

As the Zen saying goes, "When the student is ready, the teacher will come." The teachers did come—other patients, addiction counsellors, social workers, volunteers and doctors. I felt honoured to be there and very at home. It was a dramatic change for me. Addiction is terribly isolating.

Many of the other clients were educated professionals in their 30s, 40s and 50s, struck by this baffling illness, just like me. And, just like me, the majority were smokers and avid coffee drinkers.

Two more pain-relieving addictions I'll work on . . . later.

Addiction Program

Homewood's focus is on addiction as a "disease of feelings." Addicts live in their heads. I think we try to drown our sorrows in our addictions to cope with our inability to communicate or deal with what ails us.

As one fellow patient put it: "We can't drown our sorrows. Didn't you know the little bastards could swim?"

The program was rigorous, our days were full. We meditated, played sports, did crafts; we attended classes, lectures, therapy sessions and 12-step meetings; we monitored our feelings and expressed them—checked in, as they say—every few hours, discovering how mercurial our moods could be.

Since leaving Homewood, I've found that frequent check-ins keep me on course. Another tool is structure: I eat regular meals and have a detailed activity plan for my week, hour-by-hour.

For an addict, the planner is tantamount to torture. We like to do what we want, when we want. Addicts have a strange sense of entitlement, and control issues that are difficult to let go of. So the Homewood program is tough—regimented, monitored, confrontational—and there is little tolerance for abuse. Attendance is taken everywhere. You're watched, questioned, busted for every falsehood; you're walked and talked through every step.

By the time I would get to my sister's place each night, around 8:30, I felt like I'd run an emotional marathon. But the day didn't end then. There was homework—writing assignments that were a good source of information for the counsellors and therapy for the patients. Feelings that I might normally have avoided and used as an excuse to gamble surfaced in my writing and had to go somewhere else and/or be dealt with.

Aside from good food, an understanding of what makes addicts tick and new habits (a former employer literally dragged me down to the gym and signed me up, for which I'm now grateful), recovery emphasizes being with others. Isolation is not enjoying your own company. It's avoiding it and the company of others. I'd always been very sociable, but lost the knack. Being addicted to instant gratification had made me judgmental, frustrated and bored because I wasn't getting "high" on the interaction with other people.

It's strange to even have to write that. For years, I worked for an adventure travel company and happily led groups of 12 for weeks at a time around the globe. No privacy, minimal time alone. It never fazed me. In fact, it gave me a buzz.

One of my biggest worries in recovery was whether I would ever recapture that feeling; whether the artificial excitement of gambling had ruined me for normal happiness.

"Yes" was the answer I got in a group session recently, "but it takes time." Addiction isn't curable, but it's treatable and the treatment demands changing old behaviours—that's 85 per cent of the battle. Abstinence is only 15 per cent. The affirmation of Gamblers Anonymous (and all other "A" groups) is, "One Day at a Time." Or even one hour or minute at a time.

Once, early in my recovery, it wasn't enough. I had a slip. Instead of "riding the urge wave" and being patient, I let it get the better of me.

But I haven't been back since.

One factor in my recovery brings me untold joy. He's a 3-year-old, 120-pound yellow Labrador retriever named George.

At the suggestion of a few people, I had put my name on an adoption list at the Lab Rescue in Oakville shortly after my relapse. They thought responsibility for someone other than myself would keep me focused, and they were right.

George keeps me fit and shows me things I missed out on: sunrises, long walks on the boardwalk, the beach in winter, and meeting new people.

When I want to gamble, the thought of leaving him alone at home to indulge in my selfish urges stops me. Instead, I curl up with him on the living [room] floor and watch movies.

Another thought that stops me is remembering how I felt nine times out of 10, walking out the doors of the casino. That's when the cold reality would hit: I had just spent hours numbed out, in strange company, feeding my life savings into a slot in a machine. By the time I reached my car, I was in a rage, full of self-loathing, frantically preoccupied with how I would get out of this mess. The 45-minute trip on the highway—at 11 P.M., 3 A.M., 5 A.M.—was dangerously long. A quick turn of the wheel into the guardrail was tempting—solving my problems for good.

Now, I've worked too hard to succumb to it again and can't afford another relapse—literally and figuratively. Eventually, there will be money in the bank again, my friends and family will be repaid and, most important, my self-worth will no longer be straddling bankruptcy.

"Now is the time to take possession of my life," writes the poet Hugh Prather, "to start the impossible, a journey to the limits of my aspirations, for the first time to step toward my loveliest dream. If I had only known then what I know now—but now I know enough to begin."

ORGANIZATIONS TO CONTACT

The editors have compiled the following list of organizations concerned with the issues presented in this book. The descriptions are derived from materials provided by the organizations. All have publications or information available for interested readers. The list was compiled on the date of publication of the present volume; the information provided here may change. Be aware that many organizations take several weeks or longer to respond to inquiries, so allow as much time as possible.

American Gaming Association (AGA)
555 Thirteenth St. NW, Suite 1010 East, Washington, DC 20004-1109
(202) 637-6500 • fax: (202) 637-6507
Web site: www.americangaming.org

The AGA represents the commercial casino entertainment industry. It informs the general public, elected officials, and other decision makers about the gaming industry. It also lobbies for and against federal legislation affecting tourism, gambling regulations, and other gaming matters. AGA publishes industry newsletters, and its Web site archives speeches and studies that extol what the organization perceives to be the virtues of legalized gambling in America.

Cato Institute
1000 Massachusetts Ave. NW, Washington, DC 20001
(202) 842-0200 • fax: (202) 842-3490
e-mail: webmaster@cato.org • Web site: www.cato.org

The Cato Institute is a libertarian public-policy research foundation that evaluates government policies and offers reform proposals and commentary. Its publications (collected on its Web site) include the Cato Policy Analysis series of reports, which include *Gambling in America: Balancing the Risks of Gambling and Its Regulation* and *Internet Gambling: Popular, Inexorable, and (Eventually) Legal*. It also publishes the magazines *Regulation* and the *Cato Policy Report.*

Focus on the Family
Colorado Springs, CO 80995
(800) 232-6459
Web site: www.family.org

Focus on the Family is a nonprofit Christian ministry working to help preserve traditional values and the institution of the family. Its message is carried through *Focus on the Family* magazine and in radio broadcasts. The organization is opposed to all forms of gambling because of its supposed negative impact on families. The Focus on the Family Web site houses many ministry fact sheets on the harms associated with gambling. Other resources such as books, videotapes, and audiotapes on gambling are available on the site for a donation fee.

Gamblers Anonymous (GA)
PO Box 17173, Los Angeles, CA 90017
(213) 386-8789 • fax: (213) 386-0030
e-mail: isomain@gamblersanonymous.org
Web site: www.gamblersanonymous.org

GA is a fellowship of men and women who share with each other a commitment to overcome their gambling problems and to help others do the same. GA is a support group that neither endorses nor opposes gambling regulation. The organization has branches in all fifty states and in many foreign nations. On its Web site, GA provides a list of twenty questions that gamblers can use to evaluate whether their own gambling has become problematic or compulsive. The site also includes the twelve-step program that members use to combat their desire to gamble.

Institute for Research on Pathological Gambling and Related Disorders

The Landmark Center, 401 Park Dr., 2nd Fl. East, Boston, MA 02215
(617) 384-9028 • fax: (617) 384-9023
e-mail: Christine_Reilly@hms.harvard.edu
Web site: www.hms.harvard.edu/doa/institute/index.htm

Opened in 2000 as a branch of the Division on Addiction at Harvard Medical School, the Institute for Research on Pathological Gambling conducts and publishes research on the impact of problem gambling on individuals and society. The institute publishes the free weekly online research journal *WAGER* that charts studies and new information on problem gambling.

Institute for the Study of Gambling and Commercial Gaming

College of Business Administration
University of Nevada, Reno, NV 89557-0208
(775) 784-1442 • fax: (775) 784-1057
Web site: www.unr.edu/gaming/index.asp

The institute offers courses and degrees in casino management and other aspects of the gaming industry. It holds national and international conferences on gambling and publishes their proceedings. The institute produces quarterly reports on current issues and trends in the industry. It also copublishes, with the National Council on Problem Gambling, the quarterly *Journal of Gambling Studies*.

Interactive Gaming Council (IGC)

Suite 175-2906 W. Broadway, Vancouver, BC V6K 2G8 Canada
(604) 732-3833 • fax: (604) 732-3866
e-mail: admin@igcouncil.org • Web site: www.igcouncil.org

IGC is a nonprofit organization that provides a forum to discuss all aspects of Internet gaming. The organization was originally formed in the United States, but government opposition to Internet gambling compelled the IGC to relocate to Canada. The IGC continues to urge the U.S. government to repeal its ban on Internet gaming and work toward a means to regulate the new industry. The IGC Web site archives news items and testimonies on Internet gaming.

National Center for Responsible Gaming (NCRG)

PO Box 14323, Washington, DC 20044-4323
(202) 530-4704
e-mail: contact@ncrg.org • Web site: www.ncrg.org

NCRG is an organization devoted to funding scientific research on pathological and youth gambling. NCRG-sponsored researchers improve strategies for the prevention and treatment of problem gambling. The center publishes annual reports, press releases, and member-written publications—many of which are available on its Web site. The NCRG also cosponsors (with the American Gaming Association) *Responsible Gaming Quarterly*, a journal related to problem gambling.

National Coalition Against Legalized Gambling (NCALG)
100 Maryland Ave. NE, Room 311, Washington, DC 20002
(800) 664-2680 • fax: (307) 587-8082
e-mail: ncalg@vcn.com • Web site: www.ncalg.org

NCALG is concerned with the rapid expansion of gambling across the United States. It maintains that legalized gambling has negatively impacted the family, the government, and society, and has promoted the problem of youth gambling. NCALG speaks out against the gaming industry in every forum possible. It also supports other groups seeking to curb the expansion of gaming. The NCALG Web site archives many articles relating to the supposed ills of gambling as well as testimony and press releases by NCLAG members.

National Congress of American Indians (NCAI)
1301 Connecticut Ave. NW, Suite 200, Washington DC 20036
(202) 466-7767 • fax: (202) 466-7797
e-mail: ncai@ncai.org • Web site: www.ncai.org

NCAI represents many Native American tribes in hopes of protecting Indian rights and sovereignty. NCAI maintains that gaming is one of these tribal rights, and NCAI members have spoken at many venues in defense of Native American gaming. The NCAI Web site houses a few testimonies given before gaming regulatory commissions and other government bodies.

National Council of Legislators from Gaming States (NCLGS)
385 Jordan Rd., Troy, NY 12180
(518) 687-0615 • fax: (518) 687-0401
e-mail: info@nclgs.org • Web site: www.nclgs.org

NCLGS is a nonpartisan assembly of state lawmakers (representing forty-four states and the District of Columbia) who meet regularly to discuss issues related to gaming and its regulation. NCLGS was a sponsor of the Public Sector Gaming Study Commission (PSGSC), an investigative body that examined the economic, social, and political impact of gaming in America. The PSGSC's final report (issued in 2000) and other NCLGS press releases are accessible through the council's Web site.

National Council on Problem Gambling
216 G St. NE, Suite 200, Washington, DC 20002
(202) 547-9204 • fax: (202) 547-9206
e-mail: ncpg@ncpgambling.org • Web site: www.ncpgambling.org

The mission of the National Council on Problem Gambling is to increase public awareness of pathological gambling, increase treatment for problem gamblers and their families, and encourage research and programs for prevention and education. The council publishes informational pamphlets such as "Problem and Pathological Gambling in America" and "When Someone You Love Gambles."

National Indian Gaming Association (NIGA)
224 Second St. SE, Washington, DC 20003
(202) 546-7711 • fax: (202) 546-1755
Web site: www.indiangaming.org

NIGA is a nonprofit organization of 168 Indian nations that are engaged in tribal gaming. NIGA's mission is to protect and preserve the general welfare of tribes that are striving for self-sufficiency through gaming enterprises. The association works with the federal government and Congress to develop sound policies and practices and to provide opinions on gaming-related issues. It publishes a newsletter, and the NIGA Web site contains an archive of testimony from tribal leaders on the benefits of Indian gaming, as well as other documents related to the subject.

North American Association of State and Provincial Lotteries (NASPL)

2775 Bishop Rd., Suite B, Willoughby Hills, OH 44092
(216) 241-2310 • fax: (216) 241-4350
e-mail: NASPLHQ@aol.com • Web site: www.naspl.org

NASPL is a nonprofit organization that represents forty-seven lottery organizations in North America. Its main function is to assemble and disseminate information on the perceived benefits of such lotteries. The NASPL Web site contains a list of frequently asked questions on problem gambling, an overview of lottery history, and a list of the various government and charitable organizations that are supported by lottery proceeds. The organization publishes the *NASPL Lottery Handbook* and a monthly periodical titled *Lottery Insights*.

North American Gaming Regulators Association (NAGRA)

1000 Westgate Dr., Suite 252, St. Paul, MN 55114
(651) 203-7244 • fax: (651) 290-2266
e-mail: info@nagra.org • Web site: www.nagra.org

NAGRA is comprised of members of federal, state, local, provincial, and tribal government agencies that are involved in gaming regulation. NAGRA's mission is to unify the standards and practices of gaming enterprises across North America. The association holds regular meetings and publishes a newsletter that can be downloaded from its Web site.

United Methodist Church General Board of Church and Society

100 Maryland Ave. NE, Washington, DC 20002
(202) 488-5600
Web site: www.umc-gbcs.org

This department of the United Methodist Church believes that "gambling is a menace to society; deadly to the best interests of moral, social, economic, and spiritual life; and destructive of good government." The board urges Christians and others to abstain from gambling, and it opposes state promotion and legalization of gambling. The board's Web site offers (for a fee) an antigambling information packet that includes position papers, pamphlets, and article reprints.

University of Nevada at Las Vegas Libraries Gaming Collection

4505 Maryland Pkwy., Box 457010, Las Vegas, NV 89154-7010
(702) 895-2242 • fax: (702) 895-2253
e-mail: dgs@unlv.nevada.edu
Web site: www.library.unlv.edu/speccol/gaming/index.html

The UNLV library houses the largest collection of resources on the history, regulation, politics, psychology, and statistical bases of gambling. The entire gaming collection can be visited at the UNLV campus, but many documents in the collection can be accessed online. The gaming collection Web site also hosts a virtual museum of artwork and other visual elements relating to gambling.

BIBLIOGRAPHY

Books

Herbert Asbury — *Sucker's Progress: An Informal History of Gambling in America from the Colonies to Canfield.* New York: Dodd, Mead, 1938.

Thomas Barker and Marjie Britz — *Jokers Wild: Legalized Gambling in the Twenty-first Century.* Westport, CT: Praeger, 2000.

Jeff Benedict — *Without Reservation: The Making of America's Most Powerful Indian Tribe and Foxwoods, the World's Largest Casino.* New York: HarperCollins, 2000.

Mary O. Borg, Paul M. Mason, and Stephen L. Shapiro — *The Economic Consequences of State Lotteries.* Westport, CT: Praeger, 1991.

Larry Braidwaite — *Gambling: A Deadly Game.* Nashville, TN: Broadman & Holman, 1985.

Tyler Bridges — *Bad Bet on the Bayou: The Rise of Gambling in Louisiana and the Fall of Governor Edwin Edwards.* New York: Farrar, Straus and Giroux, 2002.

Henry Chafetz — *Play the Devil: A History of Gambling in the United States from 1492 to 1955.* New York: Clarkson N. Potter, 1960.

Charles T. Clotfelter and Philip J. Cook — *Selling Hope: State Lotteries in America.* Cambridge, MA: Harvard University Press, 1989.

Peter Collins — *Gambling and the Public Interest.* Westport, CT: Praeger, 2003.

Eve Darian-Smith — *New Capitalists: Law, Politics, and Identity Surrounding Casino Gaming on Native American Land.* Florence, KY: Wadsworth, 2003.

Richard O. Davies and Richard G. Abram — *Betting the Line: Sports Wagering in American Life.* Columbus: Ohio State University Press, 2001.

Sally Denton and Roger Morris — *The Money and the Power: The Making of Las Vegas and Its Hold on America, 1947–2000.* New York: Knopf, 2001.

John Dombrink and William N. Thompson — *The Last Resort: Success and Failure in Campaigns for Casinos.* Reno: University of Nevada Press, 1990.

William R. Eadington and Judy A. Cornelius, eds. — *Indian Gaming and the Law.* 2nd ed. Reno: University of Nevada Press, 1998.

Kim Isaac Eisler — *Revenge of the Pequots: How a Small Native American Tribe Created the World's Most Profitable Casino.* New York: Simon & Schuster, 2001.

John M. Findlay	*People of Chance: Gambling in American Society from Jamestown to Las Vegas.* New York: Oxford University Press, 1986.
Brett Duval Fromson	*Hitting the Jackpot: The Inside Story of the Richest Indian Tribe in History.* Boston: Atlantic Monthly, 2003.
Robert Goodman	*The Luck Business: The Devastating Consequences and Broken Promises of America's Gambling Explosion.* New York: The Free Press, 1995.
Earl L. Grinols	*Gambling in America: Costs and Benefits.* New York: Cambridge University Press, 2004.
Cathy H.C. Hsu, ed.	*Legalized Casino Gaming in the United States: The Economic and Social Impact.* New York: The Haworth Hospitality Press, 1999.
Nelson Johnson	*Boardwalk Empire: The Birth, High Times, and Corruption of Atlantic City.* Medford, NJ: Plexus, 2002.
David Johnston	*Temples of Chance: How America Inc. Bought Out Murder Inc. to Win Control of the Casino Business.* New York: Doubleday, 1992.
W. Dale Mason	*Indian Gaming: Tribal Sovereignty and American Politics.* Norman: University of Oklahoma Press, 2000.
Richard A. McGowan	*Government and the Transformation of the Gaming Industry.* Northampton, MA: Edward Elgar, 2001.
Richard A. McGowan	*State Lotteries and Legalized Gambling: Painless Revenue or Painful Mirage.* Westport, CT: Quorum Books, 1994.
Angela Mullis and David Kemper, eds.	*Indian Gaming: Who Wins?* Los Angeles: UCLA American Indian Studies Center, 2001.
Dennis Nibert	*Hitting the Lottery Jackpot: State Governments and the Taxing of Dreams.* New York: Monthly Review Press, 1999.
Timothy L. O'Brien	*Bad Bet: The Inside Story of the Glamour, Glitz, and Danger of America's Gambling Industry.* New York: Times Books, 1998.
Howard J. Shaffer, ed.	*Futures at Stake: Youth, Gambling, and Society.* Reno: University of Nevada Press, 2003.
David J. Valley and Diana Lindsay	*Jackpot Trail: Indian Gaming in Southern California.* El Cajon, CA: Sunbelt, 2003.
Rachel A. Volberg	*When the Chips Are Down: Problem Gambling in America.* New York: Century Foundation, 2001.
Denise Von Herrmann	*The Big Gamble: The Politics of Lottery and Casino Expansion.* Westport, CT: Praeger, 2002.

Periodicals

Alcoholism & Drug Abuse Weekly	"State Policymakers and Providers Struggle to Fund and Treat Gambling Addiction," April 11, 2005.

Mark Asher	"The NCAA Is Hitting the Books; Ties Between College Sports, Gambling in for a Test," *Washington Post*, October 21, 2001.
Donald L. Bartlett and James B. Steele	"Wheel of Misfortune," *Time*, December 16, 2002.
Donald L. Bartlett and James B. Steele	"Who Gets the Money?" *Time*, December 16, 2002.
John Bowen	"A Virtual Pandora's Box: What Cyberspace Gambling Prohibition Means to Terrestrial Casino Operators," *Gambling Research & Review Journal*, 2003.
Guy Calvert and Robert E. McCormick	"Gambling and the Good Society: Gambling May Be Risky but Government Regulation Would Be, Too," *World & I*, July 2000.
Dennis Cauchon	"Slots Prove Lucky for Many States," *USA Today*, July 26, 2004.
Christian Science Monitor	"Gambling on the Reservation," April 23, 2004.
Jeffrey L. Deverensky, Rina Gupta, and Maggie Magoon	"Adolescent Problem Gambling: Legislative and Policy Decisions," *Gambling Law Review*, April 2004.
William R. Eadington	"The Future of Online Gambling in the United States and Elsewhere," *Journal of Public Policy & Marketing*, Fall 2004.
Economist	"All Bets Are On," October 2, 2004.
William L. Hewitt and Barbara Beaucar	"State v. Tribe: How the Indian Gaming Controversy Began," *Social Education*, September 2003.
Joshua Kurlantzick	"Gambling's Royal Flush," *U.S. News & World Report*, May 20, 2002.
Robert Ladouceur	"Gambling: The Hidden Addiction," *Canadian Journal of Psychiatry*, August 2004.
Patrick Marshall	"Gambling in America," *CQ Researcher*, March 7, 2003.
Richard A. McGowan	"Snake Eyes or a Seven?" *America*, September 29, 2003.
Native American Report	"Indian Gaming: Tribal Leaders Tell of Benefits from Revenues," September 2004.
Christopher Palmeri and Ira Sager	"How Casinos Are Hogging the Chips," *Business Week*, October 13, 2003.
Matt Richtel	"Gambling Sites Offering Ways to Let Any User Be the Bookie," *New York Times*, July 6, 2004.
Joseph C. Rotter	"Curing Problem of Pathological Gambling: Don't Bet on It," *Family Journal*, January 2004.
Joel Stein and Laura A. Locke	"The Strip Is Back!" *Time*, July 26, 2004.
Peter H. Stone	"Odd Bedfellows on Internet Betting" *National Journal*, June 14, 2003.

Heather Timmons   "Can Slot Machines Rescue Racing?" *Business Week*,
                           December 2, 2002.

Washington Times   "WTO Lets U.S. Limit Internet Gambling; Antiguan
                           Complainants See a Win," April 8, 2005.

Mark Zampirripa   "Should State Governments Be in the Lottery
and Harvey N. Chin   Business?" *CQ Researcher*, March 7, 2003.

INDEX